DEVELOPMENT

IN PRACTICE

Managing Capital Flows
in East Asia

Other Recent Development in Practice Books

Improving Women's Health in India

Sustainable Transport: Priorities for Policy Reform

Priorities and Strategies in Education: A World Bank Review (also available in French and Spanish)

Better Urban Services: Finding the Right Incentives (also available in French and Spanish)

Strengthening the Effectiveness of Aid: Lessons for Donors

Enriching Lives: Overcoming Vitamin and Mineral Malnutrition in Developing Countries (also available in French and Spanish)

A New Agenda for Women's Health and Nutrition (also available in French)

Population and Development: Implications for the World Bank

East Asia's Trade and Investment: Regional and Global Gains from Liberalization

Goverance: The World Bank's Experience

Higher Education: The Lessons of Experience (also available in French and Spanish)

Better Health in Africa: Experience and Lessons Learned (also available in French)

Argentina's Privatization Program: Experience, Issues, and Lessons

Sustaining Rapid Development in East Asia and the Pacific

Managing Capital Flows
in East Asia

THE WORLD BANK
WASHINGTON, D.C.

The Development in Practice series publishes reviews of the World
Bank's activities in different regions and sectors. It lays particular
emphasis on the progress that is being made and on the policies and
practices that hold the most promise of success in the effort to reduce
poverty in the developing world.

This report is a study by the World Bank's staff, and the judgments
made herein do not necessarily reflect the views of the Board of Executive
Directors or of the governments they represent.

Library of Congress Cataloging-in-Publication Data

Managing capital flows in East Asia.
        p.   cm.—(Development in practice)
Includes bibliographical references.
ISBN 0-8213-3529-4
    1. Capital movements—East Asia.   2. Monetary policy—East Asia.
I. World Bank. II. Series: Development in practice (Washington, D.C.)
HG3891.M36   1996   95-51265
332'.042—dc20   CIP

Contents

BOXES

Foreword

East Asian developing countries have been the beneficiaries of substantial foreign capital inflows so far in this decade. They now receive more than half of both total and private flows to all developing countries. One reason for such strong investor interest is the continued outstanding economic performance of these countries. Most East Asian developing countries maintained economic stability and rapid growth during the 1980s, when the rest of the developing world was suffering from the debt crisis; and the pace has not slackened. Other reasons for the inflow are the growing internationalization of capital markets and the broadening of the horizons of investors in capital-rich countries. A combination of rapid evolution in financial instruments, advances in communications technology, and declining returns to investments in industrial countries was instrumental in the surge in investment, particularly portfolio investment, in developing countries in recent years. Although the increase in U.S. interest rates and the negative fallout from Mexico's crisis in early 1995 may have dampened these flows temporarily, most factors indicate that East Asia will be an attractive destination for international capital flows for some time to come.

Greater integration and participation in world capital markets are natural consequences of the success that East Asian countries have enjoyed in integrating into world goods markets through their trade liberalization and export promotion policies. Foreign direct investment (FDI) flowed into these countries in response to their market-oriented policies and low production costs, and it has been beneficial for the recipient countries. It has increased fixed investment by several percentage points of gross domestic product (GDP), transferred technology, and increased external reserves. These economies have thus been able to maintain their growth rates and attract additional foreign investment. Most of the flows to developing countries in the region originate within the Asia-Pacific Economic Cooperation (APEC) forum, including the "Asian tigers."

Today, capital moves internationally in the form of an ever-expanding variety of instruments, including increasing amounts of portfolio investment. These flows create pressures to appreciate exchange rates, expand domestic credit, and increase domestic consumption more than may be desirable. Portfolio investment, in particular, has created pressure to accelerate liberalization programs in domestic capital markets. Managing economies in the face of such large external flows is more complex than before and requires greater sensitivity to external factors. How to maintain macroeconomic stability and rapid growth in these circumstances is a primary concern for authorities in East Asia.

This book addresses a number of related issues that policymakers in the region and elsewhere must face:

- Maintaining macroeconomic stability in a more complex policy environment while continuing to attract beneficial capital flows

- Managing the diverse microeconomic impacts of the growing variety of instruments in the markets

- Matching the development of domestic capital and financial markets with the demands imposed by the foreign flows

- Increasing the availability of necessary information to officials and investors so that capital markets can function effectively.

The specific country experiences in East Asia demonstrate that authorities have adequate policy tools at their disposal for dealing with these capital flows. Policymakers are also developing informal and formal networks for discussing issues of common concern and sharing information. This has proved particularly valuable in times of stress—for example, after the recent Mexican crisis. Managing capital flows is also a priority for discussion within APEC.

This report is intended to contribute to that discussion of capital flows within the region. It follows earlier books in this series that have addressed infrastructure and environmental issues (*Sustaining Rapid Development in East Asia and the Pacific*, 1993) and trade and investment issues (*East Asia's Trade and Investment*, 1994). It is my sincere hope that this report will help policymakers to see these issues in a broader context and will help to make these topics accessible to a wider audience. It is vital to the continued rapid growth of East Asia that readers understand the complexity of the issues faced by policymakers.

Russell Cheetham
Regional Vice President
East Asia and the Pacific Region

Acknowledgments

This study, launched by Gautam Kaji when he was vice president for East Asia and the Pacific Region and continued by his successor, Russell Cheetham, is based on economic and operational work in the region and other parts of the World Bank. The principal authors were John D. Shilling and Yan Wang. Important contributors were Gary Bond, Gerard Caprio, Francis Colaco, David Cole, Ishrat Husain, Harinder Kohli, Donald Lessard, Abdallah El Maaroufi, Betty Slade, Vinod Thomas, and Michael Walton. Many others provided valuable suggestions. Data support was provided by Kali Kondury. Donna Hannah provided invaluable administrative and secretarial support throughout. Paola Brezny edited the final manuscript, and Barbara Malczak was the proofreader.

Abbreviations and Data Note

ALE	Asymptotic liability-to-export ratio
APEC	Asia-Pacific Economic Cooperation forum
ASEAN	Association of Southeast Asian Nations
BOO	Build-own-operate
BOT	Build-operate-transfer
BOOT	Build-own-operate-transfer
FDI	Foreign direct investment
FPI	Foreign portfolio investment
GATT	General Agreement on Tariffs and Trade
GDP	Gross domestic product
IBRD	International Bank for Reconstruction and Development
ICOR	Incremental capital-output ratio
IDA	International Development Association
IFC	International Finance Corporation
IMF	International Monetary Fund
MIGA	Multilateral Investment Guarantee Agency
NAFTA	North American Free Trade Agreement
NIE	Newly industrializing economy
SOE	State-owned enterprise
WTO	World Trade Organization

Note: Dollars ($) are U.S. dollars throughout. $1 billion equals $1,000 million. The World Bank Group refers to IBRD and its affiliates, IDA, the IFC, and MIGA.

CHAPTER ONE

Capital Flows to Developing Countries: An Overview

The developing countries of East Asia have grown rapidly during the past quarter century.[1] This growth has been led by rapid export expansion and supported by substantial capital inflows. Initially, most inflows were in the form of official lending, followed by commercial bank lending with government guarantees, but more recently the composition has shifted toward a wider variety of private sources, often without government guarantees. Private-to-private flows now constitute most external capital flows—the bulk in the form of foreign direct investment (FDI), which also provides transfer of technology and management skills, enhanced access to external markets, and improved competitiveness and efficiency. The most remarkable growth in the past few years, however, has been in foreign portfolio investment (FPI) flows. Flows of FPI also contribute to the development of domestic capital markets, but, as recent events show, they can be more volatile than FDI.

External savings have been a welcome addition to East Asia's already high domestic saving, augmenting investment and helping to spur growth. However, in addition to the substantial benefits they can bring, large capital inflows confront recipient countries with new risks and challenges that require careful management to ensure that those benefits are realized. At the macro level, large external flows can affect an economy's competitiveness, saving, and investment performance, expose it to external shocks, and ultimately reduce its degree of policy independence from the rest of the world. At the micro level, sustained capital inflows can have profound effects on the policies of the financial, industrial, and other sectors, on the shape and regulation of domestic capital markets, and even on the extent and form of government activity in the economy. Furthermore, since not all external capital flows have the same characteristics, different types of capital flows will have different effects and require specific policy responses if the recipient country is to take best advantage of them. This book looks in greater detail at the relation between the macro- and the microeconomic impacts of external capital flows and the range of policy responses available for best managing these flows.

This chapter reviews the evolution of capital flows to developing countries in general and summarizes the findings of the rest of the report. Chapter 2 looks at the composition and volume of capital flows into East Asia in detail and examines their characteristics and sustainability. Recent experiences with capital flows in several East Asian countries are presented in chapter 3. Chapter 4 discusses macroeconomic and microeconomic issues that determine the scope for policy response in countries receiving capital inflows. Chapter 5 examines concerns about the overall environment within which capital circulates—the regulatory structure and the institutional infrastructure. The final chapter pulls the various threads of analysis together into a strategic framework, most of whose elements are individually known to policymakers directly involved in capital markets, and sets forth the challenges and the policy options for managing capital flows.

Evolution of Capital Flows to Developing Countries

The current surge of capital into East Asia represents a new phase in the evolution of capital flows to developing countries. It is the result of the liberalization of capital markets in both source and recipient countries and is characterized by the increasing variety and complexity of financial instruments. Since World War II the dominant trend has been toward an increasing internationalization of economic activity—beginning with international support for rebuilding war-torn Europe and Asia, expanding through successive rounds of trade liberalization in the General Agreement on Tariffs and Trade (GATT), and continuing through a more general removal of constraints on capital flows (This is not an entirely new phenomenon; see box 1.1.)

In its early stages, the move toward internationalization was part of an effort by the United States and its allies among industrial countries to immunize developing countries against the threat of communism. International economic activity has since blossomed and has developed its own dynamic and momentum, outgrowing the need for official nurture. Indeed, the end of the Cold War and the demise of the economic and ideological threat of communism have given further impetus to international transactions. Some nominally communist

BOX 1.1 DÉJÀ VU IN THE INTERNATION- ALIZATION OF CAPITAL MARKETS?

The international outlook currently pervading capital markets may not be such a new phenomenon. It harks back to a similar golden age at the end of the last century and the beginning of this one, as aptly described by John Maynard Keynes:

The inhabitant of London could order by telephone, sipping his morning tea in bed, the various products of the whole earth, in such quantity as he might see fit, and reasonably expect their early delivery upon his doorstep; he could at the same moment and by the same means adventure his wealth in the natural resources and new enterprises of any quarter of the world, and share, without exertion or even trouble, in their prospective fruits and advantages; or he could decide to couple the security of his fortunes with the good faith of the townspeople of any substantial municipality in any continent that fancy or information might recommend . . . .But, most important of all, he regarded this state of affairs as normal, certain, and permanent, except in the direction of further improvement, and any deviation from it as aberrant, scandalous, and avoidable.

Economic Consequences of the Peace

Modern improvements in communications, production, and transportation have rendered Keynes's 1919 hyperbole eerily prescient for inhabitants of almost any city, almost anywhere in the world today.

countries are now major participants in expanding international markets, and those in East Asia may soon become leaders.

Substantial official capital flows and trade reforms leading to growing intraregional and international trade were the initial pillars of global economic expansion following World War II. Increased flows of goods and vastly improved communications led to an expansion of multinational enterprise and sustained trade liberalization. Internationalization of capital flows followed— first to finance the growth of trade and support the migration of production to low-cost areas, and currently as part of portfolio management in a truly international capital market. As developing countries become more integrated into international flows of goods, they are being pulled into the international capital markets. East Asia is at the forefront on both counts.

The nature and content of international capital flows have changed dramatically over the past two decades. As recently as the early 1970s, few countries, whether industrial or developing, were without substantial restrictions on capital movements. Most exchange rates were fixed and managed under the Bretton Woods system, and the bulk of external capital available to developing countries was from official sources, both bilateral and multilateral. Foreign direct investment in developing countries, other than for exploitation of natural resources, was low. Developing countries were asserting their national economic interests and encouraging domestic—often governmental—control of industry. Commercial bank lending and portfolio investment were nearly nonexistent.

Private capital flows to developing countries first surged in the mid-1970s in the form of commercial bank lending, following the initial round of oil price increases. Governments of developing countries were typically borrowers or guarantors (explicit or implicit) of these loans. They often used the capital inflows to fill budget and balance of payments gaps, either to support or (unfortunately) to postpone more fundamental adjustment. International banks had a great deal of liquidity to recycle, and Eurocredits emerged as what appeared to be a low-risk way to lend to developing countries (box 1.2). The countries themselves bore the interest and exchange risk, and sovereign risk was considered minimal at the time. Net flows to developing countries from commercial banks reached their peak by about 1980 (table 1.1). Other sources of capital have become more important in recent years.

As the decade of the 1980s opened, too much lending by banks, heavy borrowing by many developing countries, and a severe tightening of monetary policy by most creditor countries caused a sharp reduction in these flows and much higher interest rates. A debt crisis in developing countries began in 1982, affecting mainly borrowers in Latin America, Africa, and Eastern Europe (figure 1.1). East Asia (except for the Philippines) was spared the worst, although several countries wrestled with heavy debt burdens. Voluntary commercial bank lending to developing countries nearly ceased, and net flows on private lending turned negative in many countries because they were unable

---

BOX 1.2   THE GROWTH OF EUROCURRENCIES

In the 1960s the Eurodollar market developed as the first large body of international capital (that is, capital effectively beyond the control of national monetary authorities) since the removal, under the Bretton Woods system, of gold as a medium of exchange among nongovernmental agents. Other strong currencies, including the Japanese yen, emerged later to expand the "Euro" pool. Because capital controls have been dismantled in the major industrial countries, indefinitely large portions of the national wealth of Eurocurrency countries can potentially become international capital, in that such funds can move across borders without any official sanction. Many large corporations and financial institutions now actively manage large portfolios as international assets. These international assets dwarf the liquid resources of major central banks and national governments. Daily transactions in fixed-income bonds and notes amount to tens of billions of dollars. Straight currency transactions are even larger; estimates are as high as $1 trillion every trading day, perhaps more.

Direct foreign investment leads the resurgence in capital flows to developing countries.

TABLE 1.1   TOTAL NET FLOWS TO DEVELOPING COUNTRIES BY TYPE, 1970–94
(billions of dollars)

Type of flow	1970	1975	1980	1985	1990	1991	1992	1993	1994
Public sources	5.6	18.8	35.1	36.7	51.9	65.5	55.0	53.0	48.6
Official development assistance	4.8	14.4	24.6	25.5	46.1	53.7	45.3	42.4	47.4
Other official finance	0.7	4.4	10.5	11.1	11.8	11.8	9.7	10.6	1.2
Private flows	5.8	25.4	53.3	32.7	44.0	61.5	100.3	154.3	158.8
Commercial banks	2.3	14.2	32.2	8.3	1.7	2.5	13.8	–4.9	9.2
Bonds	0.0	0.2	2.6	5.4	3.0	12.8	13.2	38.3	32.2
Other	1.2	3.6	13.4	7.6	10.6	3.7	12.7	6.9	2.4
FDI	2.3	7.4	5.1	11.3	25.0	35.0	46.6	68.3	80.1
Portfolio equity flows	0.0	0.0	0.0	0.1	3.7	7.6	14.1	45.6	34.9
Total net flows	11.3	44.2	88.4	69.4	101.9	127.0	155.3	207.3	207.4

Note: FDI, foreign direct investment. Numbers may not sum to total because of rounding.
Source: World Bank (1996).

or unwilling to roll over their private debt.[2] Official lending rose and partially offset the decline in private lending. Eventually, under the Brady plan, debt relief for some of the largest debtors received official support, but it was a wrenching period for both borrowers and private lenders.[3] Toward the end of the 1980s there was widespread concern that all developing countries would face a long dry period before private capital flows returned. The scars remaining from the debt crisis, the expected high demand from investors in industrial countries, and the investment required for the reconstruction of Eastern Europe left many wondering whether enough capital would be available for developing countries.

As it turned out, the debt crisis was more an aberration in a longer-term trend toward increasing international capital flows than a watershed, and other demands turned out to be less than predicted. Aggregate flows to developing countries have recovered strongly since the end of the 1980s and have taken a much wider variety of forms. For example, the share of global FDI going to developing countries rose from 12 percent in 1990 to 38 percent in 1995 (World Bank 1996, p. 7). The reason is simple: the potential returns from investment are much higher in many developing countries than in industrial and transition countries.

The rapidity and magnitude of the resurgence of private flows in the 1990s surprised many observers. The growing internationalization of business and finance and the vast increase in the speed and volume of information flows

East Asia and Latin America have led the surge in capital flows.

FIGURE 1.1   NET CAPITAL FLOWS TO DEVELOPING REGIONS, 1970–94

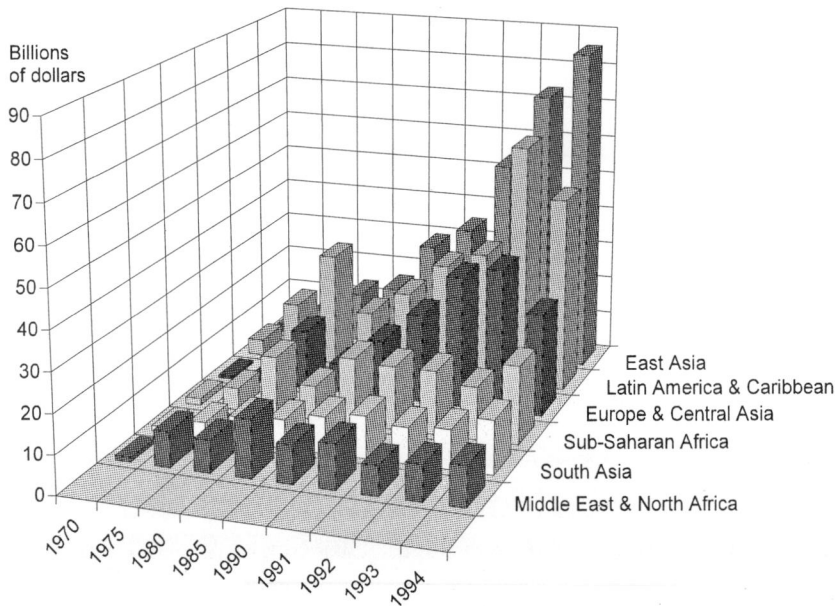

Note: For underlying data, see the Appendix tables.
Source: World Bank (1996).

have allowed much more rapid reassessment of and response to the real growth possibilities in many developing countries. And the spate of commercial lending in the 1970s, however misguided, made developing countries an object of continuing interest for international financiers. Investors in industrial countries are more willing and able to move funds internationally, and wealth holders in developing countries increasingly have international assets to place.[4] Furthermore, the volume of international flows involving developing countries creates profitable opportunities for those promoting and handling the transactions. Private flows now greatly exceed public flows in aggregate and constitute about 80 percent of total net flows to developing countries (figures 1.2 and 1.3). However, it should be noted that the surge in private flows is concentrated in only eighteen developing countries, which together received over 90 percent of all private flows during the period 1990–94 (World Bank 1996).[5]

Having borrowed cautiously in the 1970s, East Asian countries were better

The share of private flows is again on the increase.

FIGURE 1.2   SHARES OF PUBLIC AND PRIVATE FLOWS TO DEVELOPING COUNTRIES, 1970–94

Percent

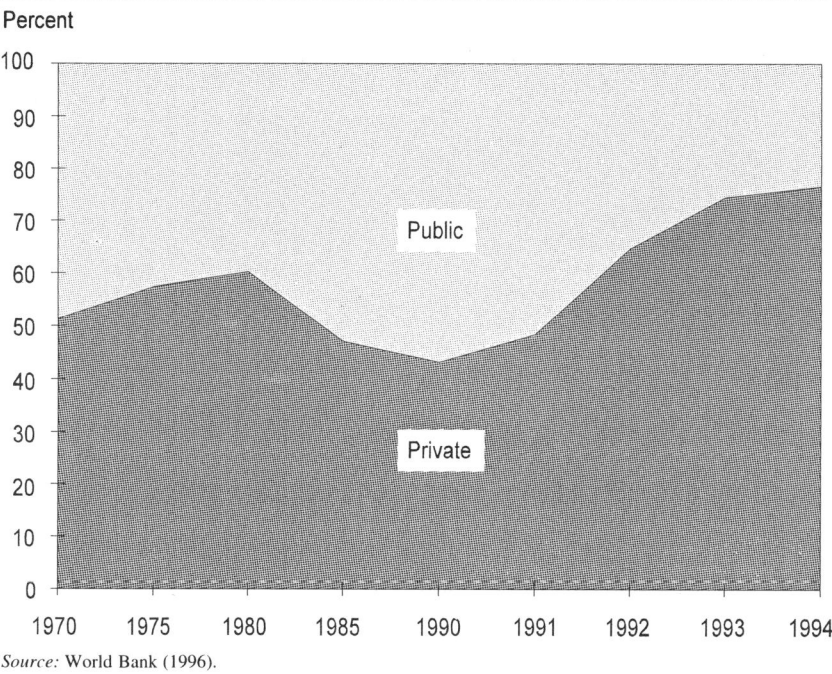

Source: World Bank (1996).

able to adjust and to ride out the oil shocks and debt crisis of the 1980s while maintaining high growth rates.[6] East Asia's good policy record, dynamic growth, outstanding export performance, and continued reliance on the private sector created a high level of confidence among international investors. As a result, the region was not completely cut off from private lending despite general retrenchment. Furthermore, East Asia was able to attract substantial foreign direct investment during this period and to maintain high levels of investment and growth. Not surprisingly, East Asia has been the favorite region for private capital flows in the 1990s. Over one-third of expected growth in world income and trade between now and the end of the century is projected to come from the region, including its industrial countries (World Bank 1994a).

The growth in private capital flows to East Asia is part of a global trend of increasing integration of capital markets. FDI grew from $1.3 billion (10 percent of net capital flows to East Asian countries) in 1980 to $43.0 billion, or 50 percent, in 1994 (World Bank 1996).[7] FPI increased from nil to $18.1

Private flows predominate in some regions, including East Asia.

FIGURE 1.3   AMOUNT OF PUBLIC AND PRIVATE FLOWS TO DEVELOPING COUNTRIES,
1970–94

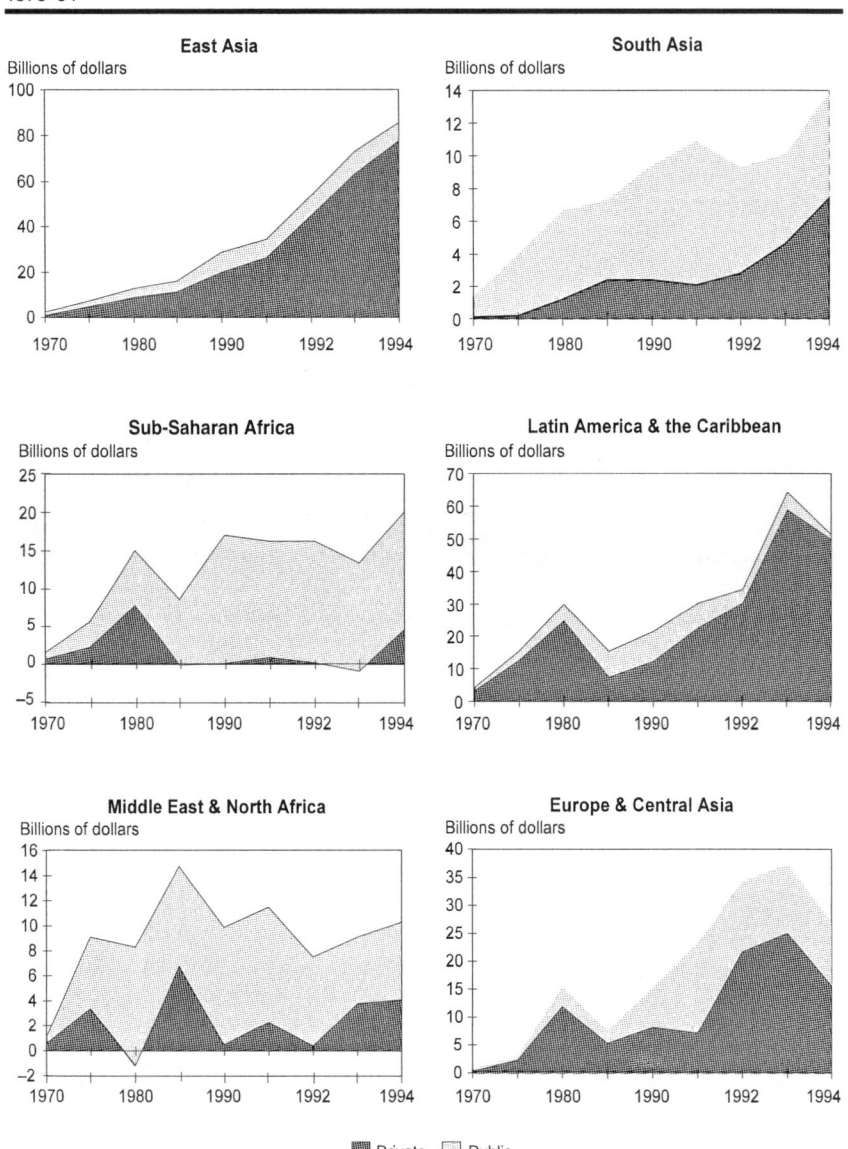

Private   Public

Source: World Bank (1996).

billion, or 24 percent of capital flows, in the same period. East Asia is now the destination of over half of total direct and portfolio investment flows to all developing countries and is expected to remain the leading recipient region. In East Asian countries these flows now represent 3 percent of gross domestic product (GDP), or 10 percent of investment, on average. Foreign capital from all sources accounts for about 15 percent of investment. This surge in private capital flows since the late 1980s has been the result of both "pull" and "push" factors—the former consisting of rapid growth and high rates of return in recipient countries and the latter of declining rates of return, fewer restrictions on foreign investment, and large pools of investable funds in source countries. Recent regulatory changes in source countries have allowed the issuing of developing country securities in industrial country markets. Technological advances in communications and financial instruments make it much easier to undertake these transactions.

There are strong reasons for believing that the flows we are seeing will be sustained, although with variations from country to country. Favorable economic policies and liberalization of investment requirements will continue to attract FDI flows that are seeking lower-cost production for an expanding list of products. These flows contribute to high rates of growth that help generate the high yields attractive to portfolio investors in industrial countries, particularly the United States and the United Kingdom. Portfolio optimization models indicate that more international diversification would improve the risk-return profiles of investor portfolios in industrial countries. The current share of international and emerging market assets is well below that indicated by portfolio allocation models on the basis of the current and expected share of these assets in world market capitalization. Accordingly, one would expect to see a period of portfolio stock adjustment that would generate sustained demand for the more attractive assets of the better-performing developing countries, many of which are in East Asia. The GATT Uruguay Round agreement to reduce protection in consuming markets worldwide will make investment in efficient export producers more attractive, and this will also favor East Asia. Although higher interest rates in capital-exporting markets and turbulence in other developing areas (such as Mexico) will tend to reduce the attractiveness of emerging markets everywhere, these conjunctural factors are unlikely to impede the long-term growth of capital flows to successful developing countries, such as those in East Asia.

The Impact of Capital Flows on East Asian Economies

Freer capital flows improve the allocation of capital globally, allowing resources to move to areas with high rates of return. Furthermore, attempts to restrict capital flows lead to distortions that are generally costly to the economy imposing the controls. Where significant gains are to be made, capital controls can be evaded and usually are, although often at substantial cost to the parties and to the orderliness and integrity of the financial system of the country involved. However, large capital flows challenge some traditional policy approaches in East Asia and have led to periodic stresses in capital markets and financial sectors. Inevitably, countries will continue to open their capital accounts and capital markets to private international capital flows. As they do, they will experience some loss of policy independence and face more risks from external shocks.[8] It is therefore important to ensure that increased capital flows, greater mobility of capital, and greater international portfolio diversification produce the expected benefits to compensate for the increased risks (box 1.3). Evidence suggests that the potential gains can far outweigh the risks but that success depends on appropriate domestic policy and its effective implementation. Prudent macroeconomic management is essential if capital inflows are to be effectively absorbed and efficiently allocated to complement domestic resources. As capital markets become more open, policy management becomes more complex. Because some forms of capital flows are highly mobile, there is now less scope for deviation from international levels of key variables. Greater weight needs to be put on achieving the right policy mix.

Country Experience

Large capital flows affect all levels of an economy. Greater capital flows into East Asian countries have brought substantial benefits: they have permitted higher levels of investment, facilitated the transfer of technology, enhanced management skills, and enlarged market access. The countries of East Asia have adapted their policies to increase investment and related imports and to mitigate pressures on exchange rates, and in so doing they have been able to sustain their high growth rates. At the same time, East Asian countries have also raised domestic saving, which has facilitated absorption of foreign capital and reduced the countries' vulnerability to variations in those flows. By contrast, for many Latin American recipients of large capital inflows, investment shares of GDP have not increased, and savings have fallen. East Asian countries, however, have discovered they are less able to intervene in their financial markets to promote industries and may have less scope for managing the exchange rate to promote exports than was the case when capital did not flow so easily.

East Asian countries have followed different paths in opening their external capital accounts and domestic markets to foreign participation. Indonesia

BOX 1.3   IF HANDLED WELL, FOREIGN INVESTMENT IS A POWERFUL TOOL FOR DEVELOPMENT

Foreign investment can be a powerful force for development and growth in developing countries, but it can also disrupt the development process if not managed carefully. Over the past three decades foreign investment has generally been beneficial in East Asia, but in Latin America the results have been much more mixed. The potential benefits and dangers listed below may apply more to FDI or to FPI, depending on the circumstances.

Benefits of Foreign Investment

■ Additional resources available for productive investment

■ Risk sharing with the rest of the world (equity)

■ Greater external market discipline on macroeconomic policy

■ Enhanced access to technology and management skills (FDI)

■ Broader access to export markets through foreign partners (FDI)

■ Training and broader exposure of national staff (FDI)

■ Greater liquidity to meet domestic financing needs (FPI)

■ Broadening and deepening of national capital markets (FPI)

■ Improvement of financial sector skills (FPI).

Dangers of Foreign Investment

■ Currency appreciation

■ Reduced scope for independent macroeconomic policy actions

■ Greater exposure to external shocks

■ Demands for protection in local markets (FDI)

■ Some loss of control of foreign-owned domestic industry (FDI)

■ Disruption of national capital markets, asset inflation (FPI)

■ Increased volatility in financial and exchange markets (FPI)

■ High sterilization costs (FPI).

Obviously, countries can obtain these benefits or face these dangers with little or no foreign investment, but the risks are greater when levels of foreign investment are high. Astute policy can enhance the benefits, and the various dangers posed by foreign investment can be managed through clear policy direction and prudential regulations from the authorities. One cannot simply assume that the market will take care of itself.

has had an open account for over two decades, but only in the mid-1980s did it begin to expand the range of domestic assets foreigners could own, as part of a series of reforms to move the economy away from heavy dependence on oil exports. Chronically high interest rates led to short-term capital inflows as authorities liberalized the financial sector. These inflows resulted in high sterilization costs, and the government had to tighten fiscal policy to dampen the economy.

Malaysia and Thailand liberalized their capital accounts during the 1980s and attracted large amounts of FDI. They have been able to absorb these flows effectively without exchange rate appreciation through a combination of policies that liberalized imports and tightened their fiscal stances. But these two countries have also been exposed to market pressures that have called for judicious intervention by the authorities.

The Philippines began liberalizing capital flows in the 1970s, but it was caught with excessive debt levels in the 1980s because it had been less successful than its neighbors in promoting growth and exports. It was the only East Asian country to go through a formal debt workout with commercial banks, which delayed its development for nearly a decade.[9] It is now beginning to recover and is continuing its capital market liberalization program. The Republic of Korea has been much more cautious, opening its capital account and market to foreigners only after it had achieved a relatively high per capita income. It encouraged the development of its domestic capital markets before opening those markets to foreigners.

China has undergone the greatest adjustment. It has been reforming and liberalizing its capital markets while engineering a transition to a market-based economy. Its capital account is porous, if not open. The reform process, although not entirely smooth, has a clear and positive direction.

Countries in earlier stages of development should encourage high domestic saving and investment habits and concentrate on attracting FDI for competitive (not protected) markets. Once domestic capital markets and their regulatory structures have had a chance to take root and promote effective capital allocation, there is more scope for liberalization of portfolio investment. It is to the credit of policymakers in East Asian countries that they have learned from experience while continuing to liberalize and have developed a network for sharing experiences.

Macro- and Microeconomic Effects of Capital Flows

Large inflows of capital can create pressures that lead to inflation, real appreciation of the exchange rate, lower domestic saving, and a reduction in the domestic interest rate or the cost of capital generally. The impact depends on the volume of flows, the macroeconomic policy framework, the microstructure of the flows, and incentives in the financial sector. The more the economy can direct capital flows into increased productive investment, the less effect the flows will have on interest and exchange rates. Governments can also sterilize the flows through monetary intervention, although usually at some cost. This practice has generally proved difficult to sustain, but it can provide some leeway during which other policies can be put in place.

The balance between monetary and fiscal policy is a critical factor in managing capital flows. One long-run option that several countries have adopted is to mobilize greater public savings. This approach reduces demand pressures on domestic resources and allows an easier monetary stance and lower interest rates, lessening the pull of high interest rates on short-term capital inflows. That governments have not typically run sustained deficits in East Asia has contributed to a favorable climate for foreign investment. An increase in public saving influences the level of public expenditures, particularly public investment. The demand for infrastructure in the region is large, and, despite expectations that private sources will provide a large part of the required funding, governments will still have to finance the bulk of infrastructure investment. Governments will need to develop long-term strategies to manage capital flows, taking into account the sectoral and distributional aspects of the flows, as well as the aggregate macroeconomic effects on both monetary and fiscal policy. In recent experience, a tighter fiscal stance has proved more effective than tight monetary policy (high interest rates) in managing capital flows in the medium term.[10] This approach has also been consistent with high rates of domestic saving and investment.

The capital flows themselves are not monolithic but represent a variety of different instruments, maturities, and risks to the country. The substantial changes in the kinds of instruments underlying these flows have important implications for policymaking. East Asia has traditionally been a major recipient of FDI, and there have been large flows between countries within the region. More recently, FPI has surged. Experience has shown that direct investment is more likely than portfolio investment to go into new projects, increasing demand in capital goods markets and for capital imports. The pressure to appreciate the exchange rate will be eased if the current account is allowed to run a larger deficit to effect the real transfer of resources, which may be facilitated by further trade liberalization.

Portfolio investment poses its own problems, which vary depending on whether the instrument is placed abroad or in the domestic capital market. Portfolio investment placed abroad may act more like direct investment if the resulting inflow is used for new investment. But firms seeking financing abroad may undermine domestic monetary policy, and large inflows may disturb a country's capital markets in other ways. Portfolio investment that goes directly into the domestic capital market may be more worrisome, as it can lead to asset inflation and thus tend to reduce domestic saving rather than to increase investment. It is also more likely to affect the exchange rate and to be volatile because it is much more liquid and more sensitive to short-run external factors such as interest rate movements. Portfolio investment therefore adds urgency to regulatory and prudential reform programs. Well-functioning domestic capital markets make managing portfolio flows easier. Although these phenomena are too new to permit hard conclusions, recent experiences in East Asia and Latin America indicate that portfolio flows can be disruptive and that governments may be forced to take strong short-term action.

The fundamentals justify both FDI and FPI in East Asia, supporting the belief that the increase in flows is structural and that fluctuations are transitory. Nevertheless, market perceptions can change rapidly, requiring continual vigilance to ensure that domestic policies remain sound. Even if a country's own policies are exemplary, external events can trigger sharp market reactions, as witnessed by the fallout on East Asia from Mexico's problems. The issue is not whether capital flows are good or bad; the challenge is to conduct both macro- and microeconomic policy so as to ensure that the additional resources provided by foreign capital inflows are used to promote growth and development.

Foreign direct and equity investments offer a degree of risk sharing with foreign investors, with correspondingly higher expected returns. Large volumes of mobile funds seeking profitable investments provide fertile ground for speculators and arbitrageurs seeking to profit from distortions in risk-adjusted yields across markets and countries. This factor imposes a great deal of discipline on national financial markets and their underlying economic policies. The more a country becomes integrated into the international market, the less room it has for distortions in major policy variables (such as interest rates and exchange rates) that deviate from the norms expected by the international financial community.[11] Furthermore, there will be pressure toward conformity with international standards for policies and regulations in domestic capital markets and other sectors exposed to external markets. All this should encourage sound overall policy. However, markets can also overreact, and countries must be prepared to protect themselves from specific, short-term runs unrelated to the fundamentals. The difficulty is to know when this is the case and when fundamental adjustment is called for.

Regulatory Implications of Capital Flows

As East Asian countries have become more integrated into global markets, their domestic capital markets have had to adjust to international norms and practices, albeit at varying paces. Moreover, governments are finding that they need to rely to a greater extent on indirect policy tools. Much of the effectiveness of these instruments depends on the sound functioning and the depth of local capital markets. Most capital markets in the region, particularly bond markets, are still in an early stage of development. They lack depth and liquidity and are subject to many imperfections. In addition, domestic capital markets have been largely insulated from international markets and subject to a variety of controls. These markets have been small in relation to global markets, but rapid changes are taking place; equity markets in Korea, Malaysia, and Thailand now rank among the top twenty in the world. As the markets continue to expand, so will the need for more readily available information and for effective prudential regulations that minimize market distortions. Reform and liberalization of these markets will be necessary to promote the orderly absorption of foreign capital, particularly portfolio investment and short-term money market flows.

Direct controls that have been popular in the past, such as those on interest rates or ownership, impede capital flows, may cause flows to be misallocated, and cannot be maintained as capital accounts open. When direct controls are reduced, enhanced disclosure, better accounting standards, and stronger prudential regulation become indispensable partners to the liberalization process. Capital market regulations or practices that amount to implicit or explicit government guarantees or insurance (against sharp declines in equity value, bank failure, or sharp exchange rate changes) tend to encourage uneconomic risk taking and speculation by national and foreign investors that can be costly to governments. Financial sector legislation needs to be designed to encourage and reward prudent behavior by financial agents. Allowing greater portfolio diversification by banks, encouraging contractual saving, and expanding options for other asset holders are important elements of financial sector reform. The development of effective prudential regulations and an efficient transaction infrastructure in capital markets (and in the financial sector in general) is as essential as appropriate macroeconomic policy for managing capital flows.

Toward a Framework

Dealing with substantial flows of foreign capital is a difficult and complex task, particularly when flows are volatile. Industrial countries have been wrestling with the issue for some time, with mixed success. Country strategies will have to adjust to individual situations, using a variety of less-than-perfect instruments. Faced with persistent pressure from external capital markets, developing countries in East Asia will have to adjust their long-term policy frameworks to accommodate flows in a sustainable way. This will involve action on fiscal policy, trade policy, regulation and development of the financial sector, and investment policy, as well as monetary and exchange rate policy. Although the emphasis should be on medium-to-long-term policies, policymakers will also have to consider the management of transitions and short-term surges. These short-term events can threaten long-term strategy and will require nondistorting interventions designed to mitigate their effects without sending mixed signals on policy fundamentals. Such interventions, which should be of short duration, are likely to become less frequent as capital markets mature. The critical objective is not just to react to short-run surges but to manage the economy in a way that will encourage stable long-term flows.[12]

In assessing the potential impact of large-scale capital inflows, policymakers need to take into account the durability of the inflows so that they can develop and implement policies to manage the flows. Are the flows witnessed in recent years *sustainable?* (Will the high levels of capital inflows continue for a prolonged period?) Are the flows *reversible?* (Will they stop coming in, or perhaps flow out again?) And are they *volatile?*[13] (Will the amounts change rapidly up or down?) Because these questions are influenced by global events and decisions in the major economies, the answers lie in part beyond the control of policymakers in East Asia. Authorities therefore must be more sensitive than in the past to external factors and be prepared to react quickly. But they can do much to enhance the durability of beneficial capital flows, both in their macroeconomic policy stance and in a number of microeconomic policy areas that affect the productive allocation of capital inflows. Planning carefully, honing appropriate policy instruments, establishing credibility, and sending clear signals are important in managing capital flows.

Sound macroeconomic policy is, of course, fundamental. That "old-time religion" of low inflation, a balanced fiscal stance, and prudent credit creation regains some of its luster as countries become more integrated into world capital markets. Most of these guidelines were developed in an earlier period of free capital flows under the gold and gold exchange standards (at least for the part of the world that participated), so their relevance is not surprising.

At a strategic level, managing capital flows becomes an issue for countries that have structured their economies so as to achieve real growth rates which generate real rates of return high enough to attract foreign capital.[14] To achieve a desirable and sustainable rate of foreign capital inflows, a country must ensure that interest rates are consistent with international rates adjusted for risk and expected exchange rate movements. The exchange rate is also a function of export promotion policy. Fiscal and trade policy should be set to accommodate the real transfer of foreign capital and limit demand-driven inflationary pressure domestically. This policy framework should seek to promote high domestic saving rates and investment in productive activities, rather than rent-seeking behavior. Trade openness is important, to improve absorption of capital inflows in the short run and to develop foreign exchange earning capacity that will enable eventual repayment. Liberalization and reform of domestic goods and capital markets will be necessary concomitants of adapting to more open capital flows externally and will increase the growth potential of the recipient country. As countries become richer, the scope for nationals to invest abroad should be expanded. This will help balance large capital inflows and increase portfolio yields to nationals. The mix of policies within this strategic framework will evolve over time as the country develops and the external environment changes.

At a tactical level, countries still have to deal with fluctuations and potentially sharp movements in capital flows in response to external shocks. They must also be able credibly to implement changes in their strategic policy stances. To modulate capital flows, countries may resort to sterilization policies, use wider bands for exchange rate interventions, change reserve requirements on foreign deposits, adjust short-term interest rates, or impose a variety of taxes or fees—or even temporary direct controls—on short-term foreign transactions. Because these latter interventions can easily become distorting and can lead to potentially costly evasion, they should be used only in an emergency. If the need for them continues, there is good reason to suspect that more fundamental policy problems must be addressed.

In sum, the challenges for East Asian countries are to manage the transition to more open capital markets and dynamic international capital flows so that capital is used effectively; to develop more efficient domestic capital markets that will absorb foreign investment without excessive risk and volatility; to allow nationals the benefits of participating in the global capital market; and to minimize the pain of transition. In the nineteenth century a massive movement of capital from Europe to America led to a dramatic shift in the center of economic power. The current movement of capital from the Western economic powers to East Asia may signal a similar event at the end of this century.

Notes

1. In this book "East Asia" refers to the developing economies of China, Indonesia, the Republic of Korea, Laos, Malaysia, Mongolia, Papua New Guinea, the Philippines, Thailand, and Viet Nam, which are included in the totals for the region. Hong Kong, Singapore, and Taiwan (China) also play an active role in the region, but neither they nor the industrial countries of Australia, Japan, and New Zealand are included in the regional totals, except as specified.

2. Repeated rescheduling agreements led to some "involuntary lending" to sustain debtors until a more lasting solution could be found. This shows up as new flows in the data on net flows in table 1.1.

A few countries, including Korea, Malaysia, and Thailand, voluntarily accelerated repayments of some debts out of current account surpluses or other capital flows during the late 1980s.

3. The Brady plan (launched in 1989) provided a means for debtors to renegotiate unserviced debt with creditors and convert most of it to bonds with lower face value or interest but enhanced security. Clearance of delinquent debt opened up the possibility for debtors to return to capital markets (although few were expected to do so soon) and generated speculative interest in the Brady bonds themselves. See Cline (1995) for a thorough review of the debt crisis.

4. The more readily domestic currency can be converted into foreign exchange, the easier it is for nationals to acquire international assets. With full capital account convertibility, the distinction between domestic and foreign assets becomes vanishingly small.

5. The largest recipients of private flows were the following (East Asian countries are in italics): *China* (24 percent), Mexico (12.4 percent), *Korea* (7.2 percent), the former Soviet republics (7.1 percent), Argentina (6.6 percent), *Malaysia* (6.0 percent), Portugal (5.7 percent), Brazil (4.7 percent), *Thailand* (4.0 percent), Turkey (3.3 percent), Venezuela (2.5 percent), Hungary (2.3 percent), Islamic Republic of Iran (2.2 percent), India, Chile, *Indonesia, Philippines,* and Poland (all between 1 and 2 percent).

6. The exception was the Philippines, which was unable to maintain high growth rates during the 1980s and suffered from the debt crisis. It now appears to be getting back on track.

7. China received more FDI inflows than the United States in 1993 and only slightly less in 1994.

8. The earlier opening of trade policy had similar effects in goods markets but quite positive net effects on growth.

9. Vietnam is currently negotiating a debt workout with commercial banks on debt acquired before it liberalized its economy. Fortunately, its debt burden has not had the debilitating effect on growth experienced by other countries.

10. Changes in short-term interest rates may be effective in curtailing short-term surges of capital in or out, as occurred following the Mexican crisis in early 1995.

11. The recent experiences of the European currencies and the dollar indicate the influence financial markets have on the national monetary policies of even the most industrialized countries.

12. Whatever instruments are traded, the distinction between short term and long term is less an issue of an instrument's nominal maturity than of the willingness of investors to sustain or increase their net exposure.

13. It is useful to distinguish between *volatility*, which is a measure of short-term fluctuation around a mean or trend, and *reversibility*, which refers to a discrete cessation of inflow—or even an outflow—in response to a shock of some sort. The former makes short-run management difficult. The latter can cause serious economic disruption if it is unexpected and unmitigated.

14. If a country is experiencing large capital inflows without having high-yield real investment opportunities, this may be a warning signal about the speculative nature of the capital flows and a reason for some kind of control until the economic fundamentals are in better shape.

CHAPTER TWO

Capital Flows to East Asia

East Asia's total debt to both public and private sources has burgeoned in the 1990s. By the end of 1994 it had risen to an estimated $415 billion, up 14 percent over the previous year.[1] The stock of foreign asset holding that has resulted from past FDI is much harder to estimate. Cumulative net flows of FDI since 1980 are about $150 billion, but there are no estimates of the current value of those assets. Portfolio equity net flows amounted to nearly $50 billion through 1994. Thus a rough estimate of the total external liabilities of the region would be something over $600 billion, which would include some intraregional obligations. East Asian countries receive substantial official flows, but historically they have been less reliant on these flows than other regions. Official flows amounted to about 0.7 percent of GDP per year in aggregate for the region, but with considerable variation by country. A number of economies in East Asia are likely to "graduate" from eligibility for most official flows by the end of the century. Hong Kong, Korea, Singapore, and Taiwan (China)— the "Asian tigers"—already are no longer eligible. Among the low-income economies, which still constitute the bulk of the region, official flows are likely to continue to play an important role, particularly for the economies in transition.

The exciting story in East Asia is the dramatic increase in private capital inflows (see table 2.1), not only in absolute terms but also in relation to GDP and investment. These flows are much more differentiated than the commercial

Private capital is the largest source of external funds in East Asia.

TABLE 2.1   CAPITAL FLOWS TO EAST ASIA BY TYPE, 1970–94
(billions of dollars)

Type of flow	1970	1975	1980	1985	1990	1991	1992	1993	1994
Public sources	1.4	2.5	4.2	4.8	8.4	8.4	8.7	10.3	8.0
Official development									
assistance	1.3	1.7	2.4	2.8	7.7	5.7	5.8	6.1	6.8
Other official finance	0.1	0.7	1.8	2.0	0.7	2.8	3.0	4.2	1.2
Private flows	0.8	4.7	8.9	10.9	20.4	26.1	44.7	62.9	77.3
Commercial banks	0.5	2.8	5.0	1.1	4.7	6.0	8.8	–3.9	3.4
Bonds	0.0	0.0	0.2	4.3	0.2	3.3	2.8	8.5	13.2
Other private	0.1	0.8	2.3	2.2	2.3	1.9	6.3	2.3	5.1
FDI	0.3	1.0	1.3	3.2	11.0	13.9	21.7	37.9	43.0
Portfolio equity flows	0.0	0.0	0.0	0.1	2.3	1.0	5.1	18.1	12.6
Total net flows	2.2	7.2	13.2	15.7	28.9	34.5	53.4	73.2	85.3

Note: FDI, foreign direct investment. Numbers may not sum to total because of rounding.
Source: World Bank (1996).

bank lending of the 1970s and are less likely to be used simply to fill budget or balance of payments gaps. The instruments themselves can have quite complex features, and the extent and diversity of capital flows now argue for a much more disaggregated approach to their analysis and management. The rest of this chapter will look at the various types of capital flowing into East Asia.

The current high volume of foreign private capital flows into East Asia is concentrated in direct investment, as has been the case since the mid-1980s.[2] In East Asia these flows tend to augment rather than replace already high domestic investment rates (about 30 percent in most of the countries in the region). The additional resources—financial, managerial, and technical—have helped sustain high growth rates. This experience differs from that of Latin America, where increased foreign capital has not generally raised investment rates but, rather, has displaced domestic saving (see Bercuson and Koenig 1993). Capital flows have been large in East Asia in relation to investment levels in most recipient countries, adding a substantial amount of resources. On average, over the 1990–93 period net capital inflows have amounted to between 4 and 30 percent of gross domestic investment (table 2.2). The averages are affected by the surge in flows in 1993; 1994 has seen some easing of these flows.

The low share of foreign capital investment in Korea reflects that country's reluctance to allow foreign investment and its modest external borrowing requirement. There is a large potential external demand for investment in Korea, representing a ready supply of capital, as indicated by the popularity of new

Foreign investment constitutes a significant share of domestic investment.

TABLE 2.2   CAPITAL FLOWS AS A PERCENTAGE OF GROSS DOMESTIC INVESTMENT (GDI), 1990–93

Country	Total flows		Private flows	
	1990–92	*1991–93*	*1990–92*	*1991–93*
China	10.2	15.1	8.5	13.1
Indonesia	16.9	18.8	9.0	11.4
Korea, Rep. of	4.1	6.1	4.1	6.3
Malaysia	22.4	29.3	20.9	29.3
Philippines	14.1	16.8	1.3	4.8
Thailand	11.9	11.2	11.6	10.5

Note: Percentages reflect a three-year average. Data for 1994 were not available.
Source: Calculated from World Bank (1994b) and World Bank database.

Korean investment funds now that the country has begun to open its market to foreign investors. The much smaller share of foreign capital in the Philippines is an effect of that country's debt crisis, which made it more difficult to attract private investors until the reform program began to produce tangible results. In the past two years a workout of the commercial bank debt has been achieved, and macroeconomic reforms have begun to take hold. Private sources surpassed public sources as the origin of most capital flows in 1993. Malaysia has been highly successful in attracting foreign flows to support its growth.

The magnitude of these capital flows is remarkable. However, not all inflows of foreign private capital have been absorbed into increased investment. Certain countries have received more capital inflows than required to fund the excess of domestic investment over domestic saving, which in aggregate is equal to the current account deficit. This "overfinancing" initially showed up in reserves, which shot up by about $90 billion between 1989 and 1993 for the countries listed in table 2.3. The increase in reserves has been the result of explicit sterilization actions on the part of central banks and of increased private holding of foreign assets in the banking system (where allowed). These reserves represent both an indicator of the strength of these economies and a potential threat to macroeconomic stability if they lead to undue credit expansion.

Major Components of Capital Flows

All types of private capital have contributed to the recent flows into East Asian countries, as was shown in table 2.1. These countries remain attractive for commercial bank lending but have avoided overusing this source. The bulk of

Private capital flows dominate in most parts of the world.

FIGURE 2.1   NET PRIVATE CAPITAL FLOWS TO DEVELOPING REGIONS, 1970–94

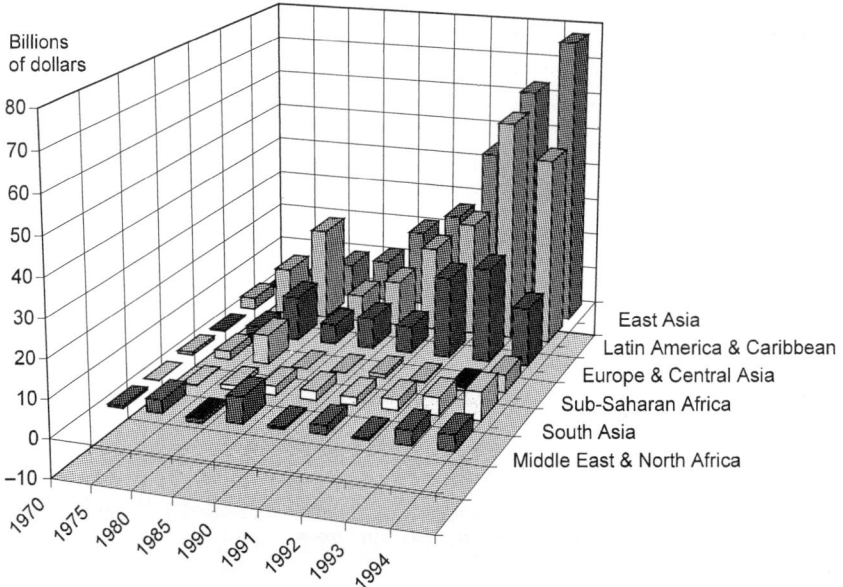

Note: For underlying data, see the Appendix tables.
Source: World Bank (1996).

Capital inflows have overfinanced domestic resource requirements in East Asia.

TABLE 2.3   INDICATIONS OF OVERFINANCING, AVERAGE, 1989–93
(percentage of GDP)

Country	Gross domestic investment	Gross national saving	Current account deficit	Net capital flows	Increase in reserves, 1989–93
China	38.0	38.8	0.9	5.3	1.3
Indonesia	30.0	27.8	–2.2	4.9	1.2
Korea, Rep. of	36.1	35.4	–0.7	1.5	0.5
Malaysia	33.0	29.6	–3.4	8.0	8.9
Philippines	22.3	18.4	–4.0	3.9	1.7
Thailand	39.8	33.6	–6.2	5.1	4.0
Average	33.2	30.6	–2.6	4.8	2.9

Source: World Bank Group estimates.

the capital inflow has been in FDI, which is most favorable for the recipient countries, since it is most likely to create additional investment.[3] Recently, the biggest increases have been registered in FPI—both equity and fixed-income securities—although these levels remain below that of FDI (figure 2.1). The increase in FPI reflects institutional investors' growing confidence in these economies, but the link between portfolio flows and new investment is less direct, and potential volatility is greater than for FDI or bank lending. There has also been an increase in short-term capital flows, which are more varied in nature; they are potentially the most volatile kind of capital flow, and they are the least likely to end up as increased investment, in no small part because of the risk of maturity mismatch. What is not adequately reflected in the data is the growth of complex instruments—convertible bonds, derivatives, and packaged project financing. They may be counted in one investment category or another and are harder to sort out because of their complex and contingent structure.

Commercial Bank Syndicated Loans

In the 1970s and 1980s commercial bank syndicated loans were the most common form of private-source capital flows to developing countries (figure 2.2). Initially denominated in dollars, these loans are now available in a variety of major currencies.[4] They are typically for terms of five to ten years, with floating interest rates set at a spread above the rate on the lenders' source of funds (for example, the London or Singapore interbank offer rate—LIBOR or SIBOR). These spreads typically range from 50 to 500 basis points, depending on the credit standing of the borrower, the special features of the loan, and the competitiveness of the market. Although borrower government guarantees are typically required, this comfort is considered less protection than it once was, and some firms can borrow on their own. Loans can be for purposes of general budget or balance of payments support, or they may be associated with a project. The borrower assumes both the interest and exchange risks. As with any loan, repayment is required regardless of the outcome of the investment or the overall state of the borrower's finances. These loans can be relatively easy to arrange through a lead bank. They are not subject to a broad market test, but the lead bank must be able to syndicate the loan to other banks. Net flows on these loans have diminished as countries are repaying earlier loans and restraining new borrowing. The action is elsewhere.

East Asian countries have generally used syndicated commercial bank loans prudently and have maintained access to these markets despite high debt levels in some countries (table 2.4). When in 1992–93 Indonesia faced a potentially overexpansive spate of proposed foreign borrowings seeking public support, it established a committee to screen and regulate the volume of large borrowings so that it would be consistent with overall economic stability. At various times

Commercial bank lending is again on the rise after almost disappearing in the mid-1980s.

FIGURE 2.2   NET BANK LENDING TO DEVELOPING REGIONS, 1970–94

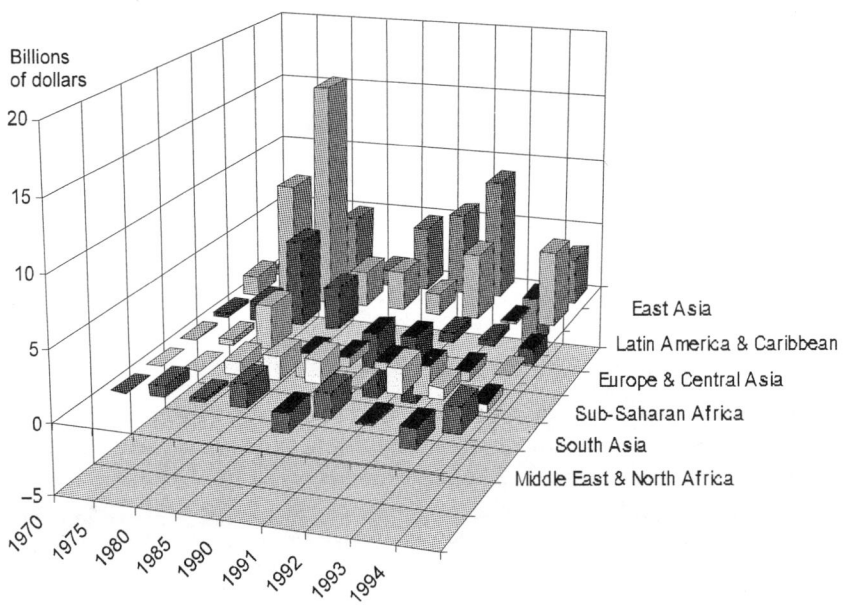

Note: For underlying data, see the Appendix tables.
Source: World Bank (1996).

Korea, Malaysia, and Thailand have used balance of payments surpluses to pay down their commercial loans. In the case of the Philippines, the net outflow on bank loans in recent years was linked to its inability to attract new loans during the debt crisis. Old loans were repaid, and no new money was forthcoming. China, Indonesia, and Thailand have generally been consistent borrowers in this market (although recent disputes between China and some lenders over responsibility for repayments may dampen banks' interest).[5] Net outflows in 1993 reflected shifts to other sources (such as bonds) for new financing on favorable terms, often with fixed interest rates. Some of the new borrowing was used to repay floating-rate bank loans. Preliminary 1994 estimates indicate a return of positive net flows to East Asia.

Foreign Direct Investment

FDI is perhaps the oldest form of foreign capital flow. Funds are directly linked to the construction, operation, or both of a project in the recipient

*Some countries have repaid bank lending when other resources
were available.*

TABLE 2.4   COMMERCIAL BANK LENDING BY COUNTRY, 1970–94
(millions of dollars)

Country	1970	1975	1980	1985	1990	1991	1992	1993	1994
China	0	0	–3	623	2,439	613	3,214	3,061	1,825
Indonesia	134	1,580	825	–318	2,573	2,428	3,065	–3,014	905
Korea, Rep. of	52	337	1,408	1,629	–589	1,952	2,753	1,241	3,232
Malaysia	3	570	716	–2,355	–389	89	993	–146	2,132
Philippines	101	282	766	532	–349	–343	–1,409	137	738
Thailand	62	86	1,234	736	1,489	2,905	1,545	–427	3,686
Total	352	2,855	4,946	847	5,174	7,644	10,161	852	12,518

Source: World Bank (1996).

country, either wholly owned or owned jointly with public or private national interests. In contrast to bank loans, the foreign investor shares the risk and benefits only if the enterprise turns a profit. The recent growth in FDI (figure 2.3) can be credited to policy reforms, investment opportunities, and expected high rates of growth in recipient economies. Low wage rates, reduced price distortions (at least for export production), and the promise of stable economies constitute the basic attraction for investors. Continued liberalization of world trade under the GATT and the successor World Trade Organization (WTO) and the inclusion of more developing countries in international trade institutions have further helped internationalize corporate horizons and increase investment in low-cost countries as part of increasingly global production processes. Changing relative cost structures and saturation in certain markets may change the sector composition and country allocation of these flows, but there is every indication that the flows will continue and will expand to new countries and products as old ones become less interesting. Malaysia and Thailand are only the most recent examples of countries shifting the product mix of their FDI-based industries as they move up the income scale, following Korea, Singapore, and others.

As in the nineteenth century, there is again a great deal of interest in foreign investment in infrastructure in developing countries, but with regional differences (figure 2.4). In Latin America and, to a lesser extent, Eastern Europe much of the investment consists of purchasing existing firms or utilities in privatization programs and taking over their operation. In East Asia there is greater interest in foreign investment in new infrastructure. The needs are vast; it is estimated that infrastructure investment requirements will be on the order of $1.5 trillion in the coming decade. These projects will create additional opportunities and should contribute to sustaining or increasing FDI flows. It should be noted, however, that most recent FDI (other than resource-based investment) has been the result of foreign producers looking for a low-cost site to manufacture their products, usually for export but sometimes for accessing the local market, perhaps behind a tariff barrier. In contrast, FDI in infrastructure stems from governments seeking foreign, low-cost producers to supply infrastructure to the domestic market. Whereas traditional FDI produced tradables (exports or import-substitution goods), infrastructure FDI will produce nontradables for a local market, often with limited competition. FDI in infrastructure—even more than manufacturing FDI in protected import-substitution activities—typically will not directly generate or save a great deal of foreign exchange. Countries will have to be sure that future total export earnings are large enough and are available to the investors for eventual repatriation. Infrastructure that facilitates the production and export of tradables, such as telecommunications, power, and transport, naturally comes to mind as most appropriate for this kind of activity.

East Asian economies have clearly increased their receptiveness to FDI, in large part because of their greater reliance on market forces and exports. They

Foreign direct investment has boomed in East Asia.

FIGURE 2.3   FOREIGN DIRECT INVESTMENT IN DEVELOPING REGIONS, 1970–94

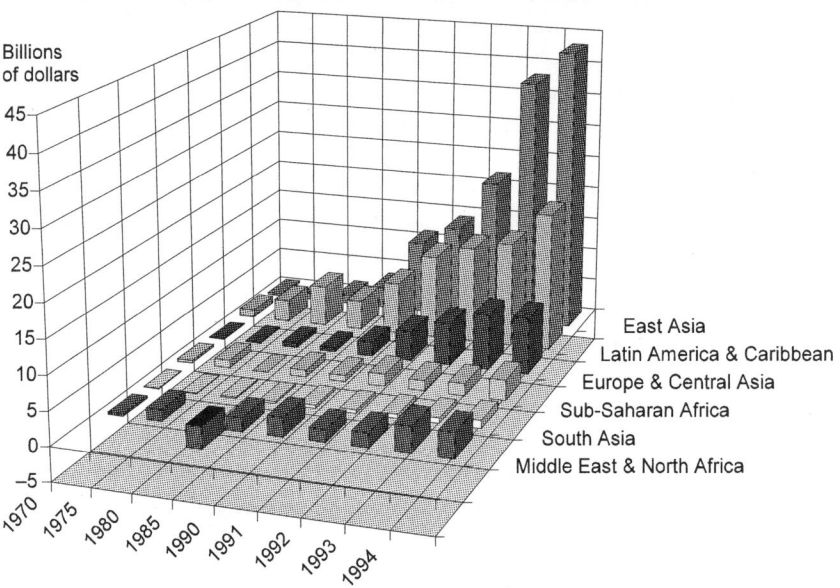

Note: For underlying data, see the Appendix tables.
Source: World Bank (1996).

East Asia's share in FDI now accounts for more than half of all such flows to developing countries.

FIGURE 2.4 DISTRIBUTION OF FOREIGN DIRECT INVESTMENT IN DEVELOPING COUNTRIES, SELECTED YEARS

1975 ($7.4 billion)

Middle East & North Africa (23%)

Latin America & Caribbean (44%)

Europe & Central Asia (2%)
East Asia (14%)
South Asia (2%)

Sub-Saharan Africa (15%)

1985 ($11.3 billion)

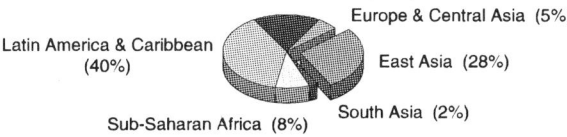

Middle East & North Africa (17%)

Europe & Central Asia (5%)

Latin America & Caribbean (40%)

East Asia (28%)

Sub-Saharan Africa (8%)   South Asia (2%)

1990 ($25 billion)

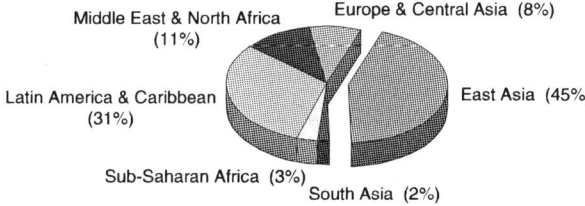

Middle East & North Africa (11%)   Europe & Central Asia (8%)

Latin America & Caribbean (31%)

East Asia (45%)

Sub-Saharan Africa (3%)
South Asia (2%)

1994 ($80.1 billion)

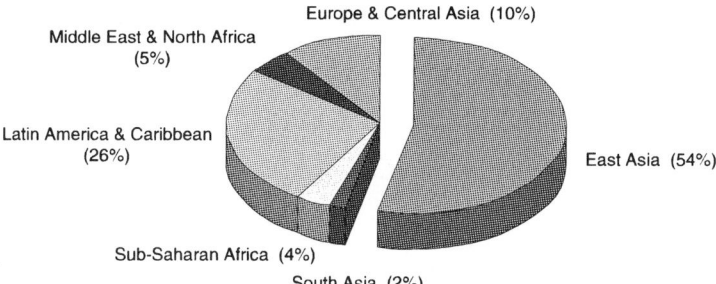

Europe & Central Asia (10%)

Middle East & North Africa (5%)

Latin America & Caribbean (26%)

East Asia (54%)

Sub-Saharan Africa (4%)

South Asia (2%)

Note: For underlying data, see the Appendix tables.
Source: World Bank (1996).

are now the largest recipient region, surpassing Latin America and the Caribbean and capturing more than half of all FDI flows (see figure 2.4). The newly industrializing economies (NIES)—Hong Kong, Korea, Singapore, and Taiwan (China)—were initially mixed in their receptiveness to FDI. The city states of Hong Kong and Singapore welcomed such flows, but the larger economies were more resistant and severely constrained foreign investment in order to encourage domestic entrepreneurs. The newly emerging countries of Southeast Asia, as well as China, have generally been more receptive to FDI, which has grown rapidly in recent years, to the point where China is one of the largest recipients among all countries (table 2.5). Former concerns that high levels of FDI may crowd out domestic entrepreneurs are fading with the development of strong indigenous classes of entrepreneurs who had often benefited from earlier restrictions on foreign ownership. Countries in East Asia now view the benefits as outweighing their former reservations. An important feature in the growth of FDI has been the expansion of clear property rights that allow foreign ownership of a broader range of domestic assets. Before this liberalization, foreign investors often acted through local nominees or partners. The Nonbinding Investment Principles adopted at the November 1994 Asia-Pacific Economic Cooperation (APEC) forum meeting in Indonesia signal a further strengthening of the region's openness to FDI. Recent actions in several countries are also encouraging in this regard.

A great deal of FDI in East Asia is related to export production, partly because of investor preference and partly because of host country regulations that have tended to direct foreign investment into export activities. This connection has had the beneficial effect of forcing such projects to be internationally competitive and efficient. In some cases, however, FDI has been attracted

The volume and growth of FDI have been phenomenal in most East Asian countries.

TABLE 2.5   FDI FLOWS TO EAST ASIAN COUNTRIES, 1970–94
(millions of dollars)

Country	1970	1975	1980	1985	1990	1991	1992	1993	1994
China	0	0	0	1,659	3,487	4,366	11,156	27,515	33,787
Indonesia	83	476	180	310	1,093	1,482	1,777	2,004	2,109
Korea, Rep. of	66	57	6	234	788	1,180	727	588	809
Malaysia	94	351	934	695	2,333	3,998	5,183	5,006	4,348
Philippines	–25	98	–106	12	530	544	228	763	1,000
Thailand	43	22	190	163	2,444	2,014	2,116	1,726	640
Total	261	1,004	1,204	3,073	10,675	13,584	21,187	37,602	42,693

Source: World Bank (1996).

East Asian countries are major investors in their neighbors.

TABLE 2.6   SOURCES OF FDI IN EAST ASIA BASED ON DATA FROM RECIPIENT
ECONOMIES, 1986–92

Source economy or region	Amount invested		Recipient economy (percentage of FDI from source economy)				
	Billions of dollars	Percentage of total	China	Indonesia	Malaysia	Philippines	Thailand
Hong Kong	21.7	34.3	62.8	7.6	3.1	10.4	17.1
Korea, Rep. of	1.4	2.2	0.4	5.7	5.5	3.3	0.6
Singapore	2.6	4.1	1.3	3.8	6.8	1.5	9.5
Taiwan (China)	6.4	10.1	6.4	8.0	22.3	2.7	8.2
Total (NIES)	32.1	50.7	70.9	25.1	37.7	17.9	35.4
ASEAN	1.1	1.7	0.8	0.5	5.4	0.5	0.5
Japan	11.7	18.4	10.2	17.6	22.2	26.4	35.6
United States	6.9	10.9	8.0	6.8	10.8	36.9	13.6
Europe	6.5	10.3	4.4	16.1	19.6	11.7	11.0
Australia	1.0	1.6	0.6	0.8	4.6	2.0	0.9
Other	3.9	6.4	1.6	2.0	0.0	0.0	0.3
			Billions of dollars				
Total, all economies	63.2	100.0	29.8	6.2	13.8	3.2	10.1

Source: Kawaguchi (1994).

by benefits in local markets.[6] Extensive liberalization in most East Asian markets has rendered such rent-seeking behavior less important, but it cannot be ignored.

It is particularly noteworthy that in East Asia an increasing amount of FDI comes from other countries within the region (table 2.6). These capital flows are often associated with expanding intraregional trade flows. A large part of that trade is in intermediate goods, indicating strong intrafirm trade and integration of production processes among firms furnishing components for final assembly. Japan was initially the hub of this process and the source of much of the FDI, but the network has become more diverse and includes many connections among Chinese and other investors as well. The NIEs have become substantial investors in recently industrializing countries. Rapid growth in the more advanced countries has raised wages and shifted comparative advantage. Rather than continue to protect labor-intensive activities, many firms have shifted production facilities to lower-wage countries in the region, often through FDI. Export quotas under the Multifibre Arrangement (MFA) may have contributed to this process in the early stages of FDI flows to low-wage countries. Furthermore, successive rounds of yen appreciation have encouraged Japanese firms to shift more productive capacity to other countries, primarily in East Asia, and the yen's recent surge will mean a continuation of this pressure.

There is evidence that medium-size and smaller firms are shifting more production abroad, following the larger firms. However, Japan still lags behind the United States in the number of firms locating production abroad.

China is the primary recipient of FDI flows (box 2.1). Hong Kong is both a primary investor and an intermediary of funds from elsewhere in the region and from industrial countries, mainly the United States and the United Kingdom. Some part of this flow is likely to be capital from other countries in the region, which converts itself into FDI to flow back into its own market and so benefit from the more favorable treatment accorded foreign investment. It has been estimated that significant amounts of capital from China and Malaysia have been cycled through offshore points to reappear as FDI. Although East Asian countries have not suffered nearly as much capital flight as have Latin American countries or the transition economies of Europe, some of the flows probably represent the return of earlier capital flight. This is more likely to be the case in the Philippines than elsewhere. There is some evidence in China, and

---

BOX 2.1   CHINA: ROUNDTRIPPING CAPITAL FLOWS

China has achieved remarkable success in attracting FDI, but some of this investment may not in fact be foreign. Rough estimates by the Hongkong Bank suggest that more than 25 percent of annual FDI flows are actually roundtripping flows—that is, illicit capital outflows being repatriated to China.

One indication of this phenomenon can be found in other outflows of the capital account. By the end of 1992 China's worldwide direct investment was estimated at around $6.5 billion, spread over 120 countries and territories (according to data from the People's Bank of China and the International Monetary Fund, IMF). Another $4.4 billion was invested abroad in 1993, making the *net* FDI inflow $23.1 billion ($27.5 billion official inflow minus $4.4 billion outflow; see the table). Moreover, the IMF balance of payment data also show that net errors and omissions (generally regarded as an index of capital flight), which were insignificant in the early 1980s, reached over $10 billion in 1993.

Where did the money go? It appears that Chinese state-owned enterprises (SOES) and provincial authorities set up shell companies in Hong Kong to funnel their hard currency elsewhere, invest in Hong Kong, or return the money to China as FDI. The capital outflows are primarily motivated by a desire to avoid exchange rate and other risks at home rather than by the desire to seek a higher rate of return abroad. China's official exchange rate fell 21 percent against the U.S. dollar in 1990, 10 percent more in 1991, and another 8 percent in 1992–93. With the unification of the foreign exchange swap and official rates in January 1994, the exchange rate risks were reduced. The exchange rate depreciated from 5.8 to 8.7 yuan to a dollar at that time. The amount of repatria-

perhaps elsewhere, that restrictions on borrowing abroad by nationals has led some would-be borrowers to bring in foreign capital as FDI but to give it debt-like assurances of repayment. This can be an expensive way to attract investment, and it shows how capital controls can be avoided.

Another factor contributing to the surge in FDI has been the growing number of privatizations in developing countries, especially in Latin America, as a major element of their reform programs, and in some Eastern European countries, as part of their transition programs (table 2.7). Fortunately, the overall records of East Asian economies with their public enterprises and macromanagement are better, so they have not had to undertake distress sales of burdensome public enterprises, as has been frequently the case elsewhere. Transition economies in East Asia have opted for a gradual process of conversion to private ownership and have not engaged in the massive privatization exercises that have characterized Eastern Europe and the former Soviet republics. Other East Asian governments have chosen to privatize to free up scarce

tion is expected to have increased significantly in 1994.

Until January 1994 China's preferential tax treatment, tariff exemption, and other incentives to foreign investors provided an incentive for domestic enterprises to invent fictitious foreign partners and repatriate capital as disguised FDI. Although China might want to relax the restrictions for capital outflows, it is clear that roundtripping is neither beneficial nor efficient for China's economic growth. Tax concessions and other preferential regulations on FDI should be eliminated. The role of government is to ensure a favorable environment for all private investment, eliminate price distortions, and level the field for competition between domestic and foreign firms. The government took further action in 1995 to reduce the special preferences extended to foreign investment.

Selected Capital Account Items, China

(millions of dollars)

Selected balance of payments items	1988	1989	1990	1991	1992	1993	1994[a]
Net direct investment[b]	2,344	2,613	2,657	3,453	7,156	23,115	30,007
Portfolio investment[b]	876	−180	−241	235	−57	3,049	—
Other capital[b]	3,913	1,290	839	4,344	−7,349	−2,690	—
Resident official sector	3,364	4,628	2,898	2,236	−3,229	−2	—
Bank deposits	1,108	−2,661	−2,135	1,655	−786	−415	—
Other sectors	−559	−677	256	453	−3,334	−2,273	—
Net errors and omissions	−957	115	−3,205	−6,767	−8,211	−10,096	−7,800

— Not available.
Note: A negative number represents an outflow.

a. Estimated.
b. Not elsewhere included.
Source: IMF (1995b).

Privatization has been much less important in attracting FDI in East Asia than elsewhere.

TABLE 2.7   INVESTMENT IN PRIVATIZATIONS, 1988–93
(millions of dollars)

Region	1988	1989	1990	1991	1992	1993	Total
East Asia	1.3	0.0	0.7	88.0	1,555.9	3,439.0	5,084.9
South Asia	0.0	0.1	10.6	4.2	41.8	16.2	72.9
Sub-Saharan Africa	0.0	13.8	38.1	11.1	49.4	544.7	657.1
Latin America and the Caribbean	213.7	183.3	2,559.0	6,718.0	3,729.5	3,392.2	16,795.7
Middle East and North Africa	0.0	1.0	0.0	3.2	19.2	302.5	325.9
Europe and Central Asia	18.9	641.2	628.4	2,083.4	3,705.7	3,153.8	10.231.5
Total	233.9	839.4	3,236.8	8,907.9	9,101.5	10,848.4	33,167.9

Source: World Bank Group estimates; World Bank (1994b).

public resources—both financial and human—so that they can concentrate on areas, such as health and education, in which government expenditure is more appropriate, leaving commercial enterprises and some utilities to the private sector. Malaysia and the Philippines have been the most active in this effort.[7] Many of these privatizations have taken place through the issuance of a proportion of the total equity in the enterprise, rather than through sale of the entire enterprise, attracting portfolio rather than direct investment. It is expected that the privatization programs will continue.

Like most countries, those in East Asia offer a number of special benefits to attract foreign capital, including assurances on repatriation and tax relief; these incentives are often administered by a board of investments. In the not too distant past, the boards often impeded foreign investment by trying to direct the flows, limit access to special privileges, and protect local entrepreneurs. As countries have recognized the advantages of foreign investment, the boards have become more active promoters of FDI. Privileges are often granted on the grounds that they offset real or perceived distortions in the domestic economy and match similar benefits offered in competing countries. Yet studies have indicated that specific incentives are far less important to potential investors than sound fundamentals, which remain the primary attraction for FDI in East Asia. (Furthermore, nationals may take their capital out and then return it so that they can become eligible for the incentives; see box 2.1.) There is little value in competing on special investment enhancements. At best they will lead others to match them, transferring resources, on average, from East Asian countries to foreign investors. At worst, they will distort investment decisions in the offering countries and blind governments to more fundamental distortions that should be corrected. (See World Bank 1994a and Kawaguchi 1994 for further discussions of the value of these incentives.) It would be far better if efforts were devoted to reducing the domestic distortions used to justify the special incentives in the first place. The APEC principles for harmonizing investment codes are a welcome step in that direction.

Foreign Portfolio Investment

Although FPI is not yet as large as FDI, its rapid growth represents a dramatic and profound step in the integration of the region into world capital markets. FDI was a result of the successful expansion of East Asia into the global goods market through exports to major consuming markets based on the exploitation of low-cost labor. The surge in portfolio investment into East Asia is a token of the countries' increased integration into global financial markets and signals a major step in their economic maturity. Latin America first led the surge in portfolio investment and in 1993 attracted the bulk of the flows (figure 2.5). These flows declined in 1994 worldwide, and particularly in Latin America. A substantial portion of the flows into Latin America in the early 1990s went into Mexican stocks, probably related to the North American Free Trade Agreement (NAFTA), and into Argentina and Brazil following the resolution of the debt disputes with international banks. The recent experience in Mexico illustrates the reversibility of these flows.

Portfolio investment can take a variety of forms (table 2.8). Investors may purchase bonds (debt) of developing country governments or firms, either in a major international currency in a major international market or in local currency in the host country market. They may also purchase equity (stocks) in either international or domestic markets. It is now much easier for securities of developing countries and their firms to be listed and traded in major markets or over the counter in industrial countries. Equity and bond investment differs from FDI and commercial bank lending in that the ultimate provider of funds is removed from direct involvement in the fund's use. Investors in FPI are buying a claim on the income streams of the issuer and are primarily interested in the yield and security of their funds; in the case of equity, investors are also sharing the risks. There is some evidence that in emerging markets the country is the major factor in foreign investor decisions and the specific firm choice is secondary (see, for example, *World Equity*, November 1994, p. 3). This implies that, as markets open, foreign investors initially invest more in country prospects in general and are less discriminating across instruments within the country. The still-limited number of large issues in most emerging markets partially accounts for these tendencies. Investors are likely to become

Portfolio flows rose sharply in 1993 and 1994.

FIGURE 2.5   NET TOTAL PORTFOLIO INVESTMENT IN DEVELOPING REGIONS, 1980–94

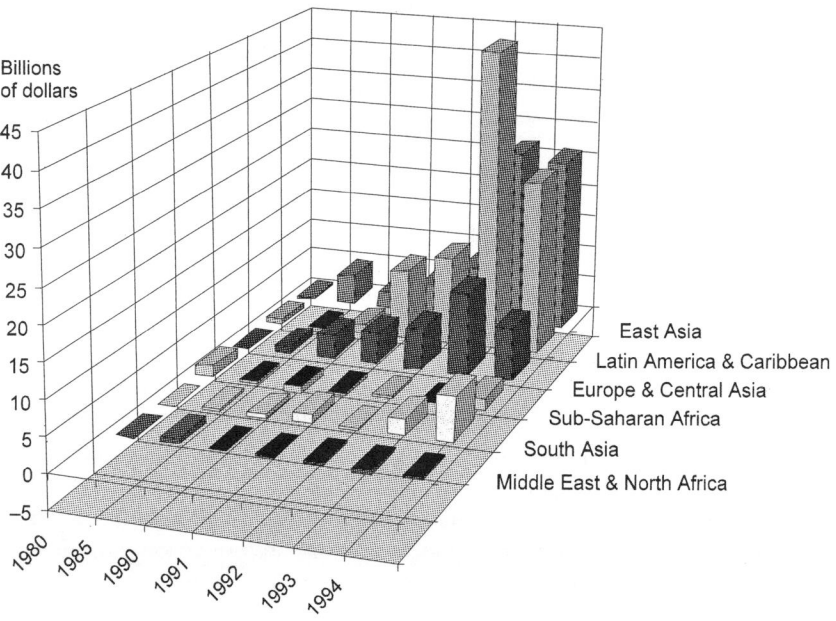

Note: For underlying data, see the Appendix tables.
Source: World Bank (1996).

Portfolio investment can take a variety of forms.

TABLE 2.8   TYPES OF GROSS PORTFOLIO INVESTMENT IN EAST ASIA, 1989–94
(millions of dollars)

Type of investment	1989	1990	1991	1992	1993	1994
Commercial paper	2,129	5,115	6,723	10,466	6,530	641
Bond placement abroad	–51	–114	1,973	1,215	3,982	17,441
Total portfolio equity flows	2,623	2,268	1,049	5,102	18,775	17,885
Equity placed abroad	0	40	205	1,452	2,963	7,800
Direct equity purchases	1,268	342	694	2,795	15,144	8,150
Closed-end funds	1,355	1,886	150	855	668	1,935
Total	4,701	7,269	9,745	16,783	29,287	35,967

Source: World Bank staff estimates; World Bank data.

more discriminating among issues as more information becomes available and more companies are listed. The growth of country funds is another indication of the attraction of investing in fast-growing countries.

Portfolio investment offers existing firms an easier means of raising foreign capital than seeking an FDI partner. The large volumes of funds available in global markets facilitate such transactions. However, since portfolio securities are normally traded in secondary markets, these investors have the option of getting out of an investment relatively easily (although perhaps at some loss), compared with getting out of direct investment. This difference has two important implications for recipients of portfolio investment. First, demand for, and hence prices of, individual issues or groups of issues may be volatile, particularly for short-term instruments.[8] Second, not all purchases of portfolio investment bring in new capital or create new investment; new issues of stocks and bonds will bring in new capital, but purchases in secondary markets, even if new foreign buyers are coming in, will not necessarily increase investment or net inflows of foreign exchange and may reduce domestic saving. The net impact depends on whether the seller uses the proceeds to undertake new investment, buy other existing assets, expatriate or repatriate the funds (if the seller is foreign), or consume. Even new issues may not contribute to additional investment if the proceeds are used to retire other domestic debt or fund current expenditures. Although refinancing foreign debt with equity results in a net flow of zero, it changes the structure of external liabilities, which may be desirable. Before domestic capital markets mature, pricing anomalies and other market imperfections may create opportunities for arbitrage and other speculation related to these imperfections, and this in turn may contribute to volatility.

The development of portfolio investment in East Asia has been varied (table 2.9). Some countries have been slower in opening their domestic capital markets to foreign ownership than in liberalizing direct investment. Others have made access to foreign markets for portfolio placements more discretionary. The former stance reflects either the weak state of development of domestic capital markets or a reluctance to allow foreigners to become too involved, or both. The latter reflects more stringent market listing requirements in advanced capital markets that have kept out some borrowers.[9]

Two principal factors have been driving the growth in portfolio investment. On the recipient country side, governments and public and private enterprises have been seeking additional funding and have often found more favorable terms and larger placements available in foreign than in local markets. Sustained rapid growth in developing countries has ensured that many firms, as well as governments, are sufficiently creditworthy to gain access to foreign equity and bond markets. On the source side, interest in overseas portfolio

Portfolio investment in East Asian countries depends on both the openness and the stability of domestic capital markets.

TABLE 2.9   PORTFOLIO INVESTMENTS IN EAST ASIA, 1970–94
(millions of dollars)

Country	1970	1975	1980	1985	1990	1991	1992	1993	1994
China	0	0	50	971	–48	677	1,191	4,516	6,791
Indonesia	0	0	40	–40	338	381	274	1,845	4,167
Korea, Rep. of	0	0	44	1,271	687	3,067	5,606	9,723	6,682
Malaysia	–30	–3	–11	2,253	80	143	11	3,745	2,296
Philippines	–1	–2	80	–71	395	124	282	1,815	2,333
Thailand	0	0	44	60	362	–36	553	4,889	3,237
Total	–31	–5	248	4,445	1,814	4,356	7,916	26,532	25,506

Note: Both bond placement and portfolio equity investment are included. Numbers may not sum to totals because of rounding.
Source: World Bank (1996).

investment has grown as a result of reduced controls on foreign capital placements in investor countries and the growing interest of large institutional investors in emerging markets as a portfolio diversification measure with potential high yields (box 2.2). In addition, the relative decline in interest rates in industrial countries (primarily the United States) in 1992–93 increased the attractiveness of investment in better-performing foreign assets, particularly those in East Asia. The 1994 increase in interest rates (again primarily in the United States) has moderated the supply push, but the decline in 1995 may again encourage flows. The expansion of the past few years, however, has probably provided enough impetus to change permanently the structure of investment patterns. East Asian countries have been "discovered" and are now regularly included in investor horizons.

Bonds

The most conventional portfolio investments have been bonds placed abroad in the currency of the lender. These are fixed maturity and may be at fixed or floating interest rates. The borrower faces exchange rate risk, and may face interest rate risk if rates are floating. Bond placements are governed by the rules of disclosure and credit standing in the market in which they are issued. In recent years industrial country markets have moved to facilitate such issues, subject to adequate prudential requirements. Latin American borrowers pioneered these placements in U.S. markets, but East Asian and Eastern European

BOX 2.2 ALTERNATIVE METHODS OF RAISING CAPITAL OVERSEAS

A number of facilities have been created to allow developing countries to raise capital in major industrial country markets.

Equity Instruments

■ *American Deposit Receipts* (ADRS) are equity-based financial securities that are denominated in and pay dividends in U.S. dollars. They are issued by banks as evidence of ownership of the underlying stock of non-U.S. corporations and are publicly traded on the U.S. securities exchanges (New York Stock Exchange, AMEX, NASDAQ).

■ *Global Depository Receipts* (GDRS) are similar to ADRS except that they are offered in foreign stock markets as well as in the U.S. private placement market and they can be traded in several currencies. (GDRS are governed by Rule 144a of the U.S. Securities and Exchange Commission, which places fewer requirements on these issues than on ADRS but restricts ownership to certain large investors.)

■ *Euroequity* issues, like Eurobonds (discussed below), are issued simultaneously in several national markets by international syndicates. The Euroequity markets began in 1980, experienced rapid growth through 1986, declined in 1987–88, and by 1989 had recovered to approximately $15 billion.

Bond Instruments

■ *Eurobonds* (a) are underwritten by an international syndicate, (b) at issuance are offered simultaneously to investors in a number of countries, (c) are issued outside the jurisdiction of any single country, and (d) are unregistered. The Eurobond market is divided into different sectors, based on the currency in which the issue is denominated. For example, when the bonds are denominated in U.S. dollars, they are referred to as *Eurodollar bonds.*

■ *Yankee bonds* are U.S. dollar–denominated bonds issued by foreign entities and traded in the foreign bond market in the United States. Similar instruments are traded in Japan (where yen-denominated bonds issued by non-Japanese entities are nicknamed *Samurai bonds*), the United Kingdom *(Bulldog bonds),* the Netherlands *(Rembrandt bonds),* Spain (*Matador bonds),* and Hong Kong and Singapore *(Dragon bonds).*

borrowers are not far behind. After years of quiescence, this part of the bond market is now flourishing, with a growing portion of developing countries' bonds carrying enhancements such as puts or convertible features.[10]

Nearly all East Asian foreign bond placements have been in U.S. dollars (table 2.10); yen placements are a distant second. This preference is not surprising—the dollar market is the largest, its interest rates have been attractive, and the exchange risk is less because a large portion of East Asian exports is denominated in U.S. dollars. Low interest rates, particularly in U.S.

Bond flows took off in three regions.

FIGURE 2.6   NET BOND FLOWS TO DEVELOPING REGIONS, 1980–94

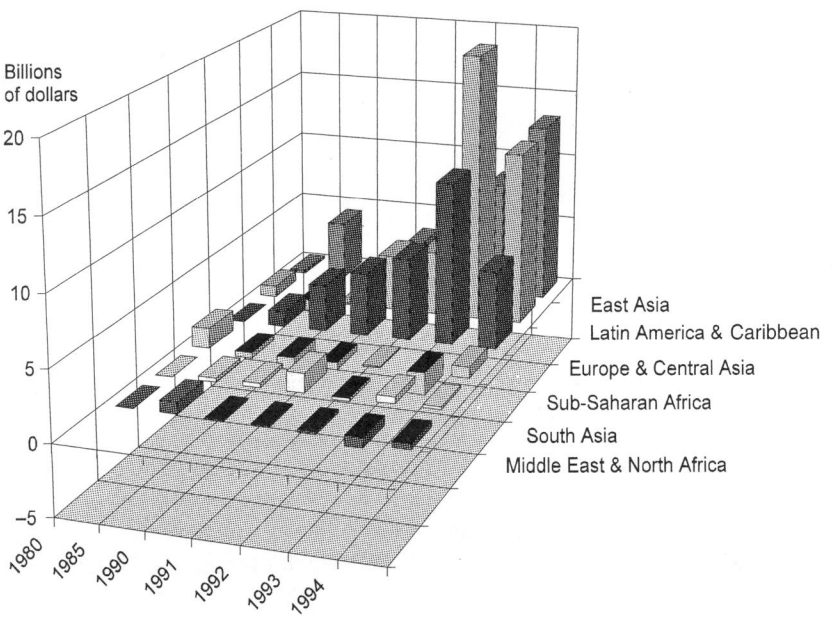

Note: For underlying data, see the Appendix tables.
Source: World Bank (1996).

China, Korea, and Thailand are the main users of bonds for raising capital.

TABLE 2.10   BOND PLACEMENT BY COUNTRY, 1970–94
(millions of dollars)

Country	1970	1975	1980	1985	1990	1991	1992	1993	1994
China	0	0	50	971	–48	24	–3	2,238	2,876
Indonesia	0	0	40	–40	26	381	155	8	495
Korea, Rep. of	0	0	44	1,177	169	2,722	2,560	3,694	4,157
Malaysia	–30	–3	–11	2,253	–212	143	–374	45	976
Philippines	–1	–2	80	–71	395	124	–52	734	926
Thailand	0	0	44	16	–87	–77	549	1,772	3,775
Total	–31	–5	248	4,307	243	3,316	2,836	8,490	13,205

Note: Both private guaranteed and nonguaranteed bonds are included.
Source: World Bank (1996).

dollar markets in 1993, offered many borrowers the opportunity to lock in favorable rates. The subsequent increase in rates made such issues less attractive, and action slowed in 1994 (figure 2.6).

There has been growing interest in bonds placed in local markets as well, although in East Asia this interest is limited because domestic bond markets are either not well developed or not open to foreigners (as in the case of Korea; see World Bank 1995). Fixed-term instruments tend to offer more risk for the return (including currency and sovereign risk) than bonds in foreign markets or stocks in either domestic or foreign markets, especially for medium or longer-term maturities. Short-term instruments have attracted some interest when domestic rates have been particularly high. In those cases, flows have been large, but it has been difficult to identify their extent among other short-term flows and errors and omissions. Flows have been considered substantial in Indonesia, Malaysia, and the Philippines at various times.

Stocks

Much of the recent surge in portfolio investment has been in the form of equity investment. Active equity markets are a relatively recent phenomenon in East Asian countries and have grown in fits and starts. A brief flurry of activity in stocks occurred in some countries in 1989–90 but was cut short by the effects of the Gulf War on international investment. Confidence has been restored, and East Asian countries have moved to open their markets. A more serious influx began in 1992 and has surged since (figure 2.7; table 2.11). On the demand side, the development of a middle class interested in investing, the interest of foreign investors, and the active promotion of stock markets by governments and market agents have all encouraged expansion. On the supply side, most corporations in the region have heretofore been closely held, but they must now address markets to expand their sources of financing. A number of East Asian companies have attained a size and degree of profitability that have enabled them to raise equity funds directly in international capital markets. Some companies must turn to these markets because domestic markets are not yet mature enough or deep enough for their needs. As in the case of bonds placed in foreign markets, equities issued and traded in foreign markets have no direct effect on national securities or exchange markets beyond the initial inflow of funds. Some corporations have issued stocks in both international and domestic markets, and investors tend to feel more comfortable when issues are also traded in their home markets.

Most of the foreign investors' interest in equities and most of the expansion in trading have occurred in the recipient country markets themselves. The development of these markets has been advanced by the interest of a number of

Equity investment is highly concentrated in Latin America and East Asia.

FIGURE 2.7   NET PORTFOLIO EQUITY INVESTMENT IN DEVELOPING REGIONS, 1980–94

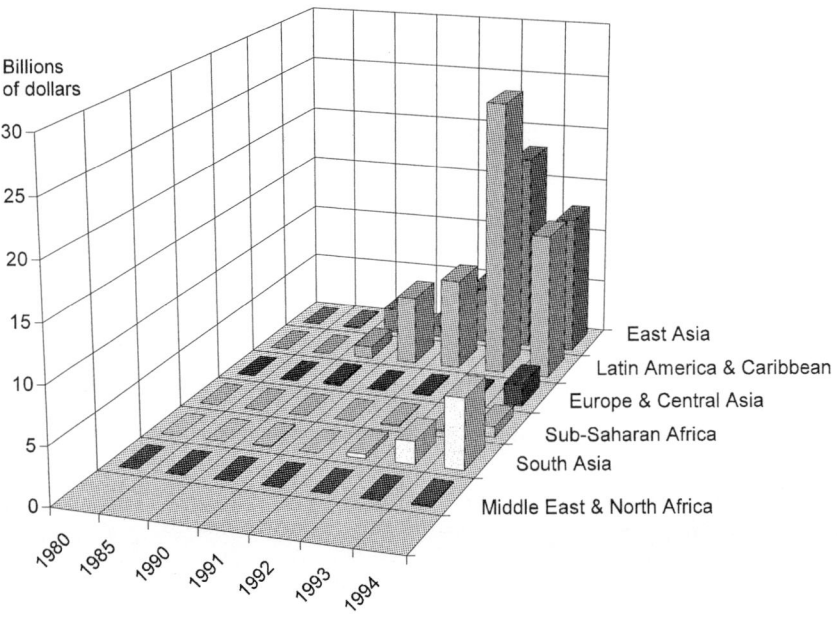

Note: For underlying data, see the Appendix tables.
Source: World Bank (1996).

Equity investment has been variable in recent years.

TABLE 2.11   EQUITY INVESTMENT BY COUNTRY, 1985–94
(millions of dollars)

Country	1980	1985	1990	1991	1992	1993	1994
China	0	0	0	653	1,194	2,278	3,915
Indonesia	0	0	312	0	119	1,836	3,672
Korea, Rep. of	0	94	518	345	3,045	6,029	2,525
Malaysia	0	0	293	0	385	3,700	1,320
Philippines	0	0	0	0	333	1,082	1,407
Thailand	0	44	449	41	4	3,117	–538
Total	0	138	1,571	1,039	5,080	18,042	12,301

Note: Numbers may not sum to totals because of rounding.
Source: World Bank (1996).

international investors specializing in emerging markets who have encouraged governments to open their domestic capital markets to more foreign participation. Speculative profits made in Latin America following reforms and the initial resolution of debt problems; the high degree of interest in the privatizations in Eastern Europe and the former Soviet republics; and the continued high growth rates in East Asia and, recently, South Asia have all fueled the interest of high-risk, high-yield investors in emerging markets (see figure 2.7). Latin America, which has been the leader in attracting equity placements, enjoyed a real boom in 1993 as investors moved to take advantage of NAFTA in Mexico and of the expected recoveries in Brazil and Argentina. The general drop in overseas investment from the United States in 1994 most sharply affected this region; investment has fallen by more than half. East Asia, however, has retained its luster (box 2.3). Preliminary data indicate at least sustained equity flows in 1995 despite less favorable conditions (for example, higher interest rates) in source country markets. Because stocks in developing countries rarely pay substantial dividends, these investors are looking for appreciation, and the sharp increases in price-earnings ratios in these markets have demonstrated this potential. Investors are hoping to get in on the ground floor of long-term bull markets.

The surge of investment from these funds into rather shallow markets has had a large impact, driving up values and trading volumes, and initially generating high yields. Market capitalization in some East Asian countries now exceeds that of some of the smaller industrial country markets (table 2.12). The number of new issues in East Asian stock markets has been increasing, partly as a function of growing interest by foreign portfolio investors. The relatively high demand for emerging country issues at favorable prices has in many cases shifted the enterprise financing equation in favor of more equity. This has been abetted by banking sector reforms that have reduced the availability of directed or subsidized credit to many firms. A substantial part of the growth in market capitalization in the East Asian markets is attributable to new issues. The number of listed stocks in the International Finance Corporation's (IFC's) Emerging Markets database is continually expanding (table 2.13).

Rapid price movement and volatility have characterized East Asian stock markets almost since their inception. There have been some wild rides, and the infusion of new outside money has made these markets more exciting. In addition to increasing overall demand, foreign investors trading in domestic markets may also introduce more volatility; they are more active traders and seek high yields across various stocks and indeed across national markets. It has been estimated, for example, that 80 percent of the turnover in Indonesia's stock market is due to foreign investors, who own about 20 percent of the

BOX 2.3   DEVELOPING COUNTRIES MUST COMPETE FOR PORTFOLIO CAPITAL FLOWS

The rapid increase in FPI flows to emerging markets has led to concerns about a sudden reversal of these flows and about the possibility that foreign investors may switch their investments from one country to another in the short run. Gooptu (1994) investigates the question of whether portfolio investment flows to one developing region are significantly related to those going to another region—that is, are the flows coming from new investable resources in industrial countries, implying independence or perhaps complementarity in flows to developing regions, or is there a relatively fixed allocation to developing markets, making flows to different regions or countries competitive?

The study employs quarterly World Bank data on gross portfolio flows for eight emerging markets—India, Indonesia, Korea, and Thailand in Asia, and Argentina, Brazil, Chile, and Mexico in Latin America—for the period 1989, first quarter, through 1993, second quarter. Results from econometric analysis show a negative relationship between total portfolio flows to Asian emerging markets and to Latin America. The study examines separately debt portfolios (bonds, certificates of deposit, and commercial paper) and equity portfolio flows (closed-end country fund, depository receipts, and direct purchases of stocks by foreign investors). The negative relationship holds for both debt and equity portfolio flows.

Thus, despite the surge of total portfolio inflows to developing countries in the 1990s, there is evidence that investors view different destinations as alternatives, supporting the hypothesis that these markets compete for portfolio investment. This finding reinforces the view that policymakers in developing countries must continue to provide the right signals to international capital markets in terms of economic reforms, institution building, and regulations if they are to compete successfully with other developing countries for the pool of private capital. In the long run, the right policy mix matters in sustaining capital flows to those well-performing economies with improved creditworthiness. The results also highlight the potential benefits of continuing substantial financial sector and macroeconomic reforms in order to maintain the sustainability of capital flows.

equity. So far, the high turnover within national markets has not led to sharp outflows. However, high double-digit returns based on initial appreciation are not sustainable. As impressive as the underlying economic and sector growth rates are (up to 10–20 percent per year in manufacturing sectors), they cannot sustain the 40 to 60 percent rates of return in equities that equity investors and funds cite as targets, as market declines in early 1994 demonstrated (table 2.14).

National stock markets are expanding rapidly in East Asia.

TABLE 2.12   MARKET CAPITALIZATION BY COUNTRY, 1984–95
(billions of dollars)

Country	1984	1988	1990	1991	1992	1993	1994	End June 1995	Growth, 1984–94 (percent)
China	0.0	0.0	0.0	2.0	18.3	40.6	43.5	42.9	—
Indonesia	0.1	0.3	8.1	6.8	12.0	33.0	47.2	52.2	—
Korea	6.2	94.2	110.6	96.4	107.4	139.4	191.8	178.7	2,990
Malaysia	19.4	23.3	48.6	58.6	94.0	220.3	199.3	224.2	927
Philippines	0.8	4.3	5.9	10.2	13.8	40.3	55.5	55.0	6,837
Thailand	1.7	8.8	23.9	35.8	58.3	130.5	131.5	150.6	7,635
Total	28.3	130.9	197.1	209.9	303.8	604.1	668.8	703.6	2,263
Japan	667.0	3,906.7	2,917.7	3,130.9	2,399.0	2,999.8	—	—	—
United States	1,862.9	2,793.8	3,089.7	4,099.5	4,497.8	5,223.8	—	—	—

— Not available
Note: Numbers may not sum to totals because of rounding.
Source: IFC (1994, 1995).

Increasingly, companies are listing on East Asian stock exchanges.

TABLE 2.13   COMPANIES LISTED ON EAST ASIAN STOCK EXCHANGES, 1984–95
(number of firms)

Country	1984	1988	1990	1991	1992	1993	1994	End June 1995	Average annual growth, 1984–94 (percent)	Period growth, 1984–94 (percent)
China	—	—	—	14	52	183	291	302	—	—
Indonesia	24	24	125	141	155	174	216	224	72	800
Korea	336	502	669	686	688	603	699	701	10	108
Malaysia	217	238	282	321	369	410	478	507	11	120
Philippines	149	141	153	161	170	180	189	197	2.4	27
Thailand	96	141	214	276	305	347	389	404	28	305
Total	822	1,046	1,443	1,599	1,739	1,897	2,262	2,335	16	184
United States	7,977	6,680	6,599	6,742	7,014	7,607	—	—	—	—

— Not available
Note: Numbers may not sum to totals because of rounding.
Source: IFC (1994, 1995).

One result of these inflows into East Asia's stock market has been an increase in the wealth of all equity holders. Higher price-to-earnings ratios lower the cost of capital for new issues and may encourage more firms to raise capital through equity, thereby deepening the market. Some companies have been able to raise equity in local markets to retire debt, and in doing so they have improved their balance sheets and reduced overall liquidity. This has also helped the liquidity of

Price-to-earnings ratios are high but volatile.

TABLE 2.14   PRICE-TO-EARNINGS RATIOS, 1983–95

Country	1983	1988	1989	1990	1991	1992	1993	1994	April–June 1995
China	—	—	—	—	—	—	—	—	—
Indonesia	—	—	56	20	11	12.2	29	20.2	20.9
Korea, Rep. of	19	39	28	16	21	21.4	25	34.5	18.9
Malaysia	30	33	27	23	21	21.8	44	29.0	27.3
Philippines	—	13	14	11	11	14.1	39	30.8	20.1
Thailand	11	11	16	9	12	13.9	28	21.2	23.3

— Not available.
Source: IFC (1994, 1995).

the banking system, but it may increase lending in other areas, such as real estate. Greater ease in raising capital might encourage more domestic investment and perhaps attract more savings as well, but the evidence on this point is sparse and mixed. To the extent that wealth is a positive factor in consumption functions, this would lead to higher consumption and lower current savings.

Other Instruments

In addition to the conventional instruments already discussed, recent innovations in international financial markets are making new financing options available to many countries. One of the most promising takes the form of integrated or structured project finance packages. These packages often include a combination of equity (possibly both FDI and FPI) and debt (perhaps both bonds and loans). They are usually structured from private sources, but official-source lending may be included, depending on the nature of the investment. These packages are typically for large infrastructure projects, where massive private participation is increasingly necessary. The private funding component is usually a mixture of domestic and foreign finance, and the structure is usually "nonrecourse," meaning that the lenders can seek repayment only from the project itself. Build-operate-transfer (BOT), build-own-operate-transfer (BOOT), and build-own-operate (BOO) financing come under the general umbrella of project finance. There is generally no sovereign guarantee from the government, but in the case of infrastructure and public utilities the government usually agrees to long-term tariff-setting rules, purchase or supply contracts, and other economic conditions related to the specific project to ensure that it is marketable. Since the government controls many of the economic factors related to the project, private investors require the government to offer certain assurances against what are called sovereign risks; the private operators bear the commercial and project risks. In some cases, official agencies such as the World Bank, the Multilateral Investment Guarantee Agency (MIGA), the IFC, or public financial institutions of an industrial country may provide insurance against specified noncommercial risks. Project financing packages may also be arranged for entirely private projects if the project organizers are sufficiently creditworthy and experienced.

The Philippines has already concluded some thirty-three BOOT projects, valued at an estimated $4 billion. Indonesia has also completed several, and more projects are under negotiation in other countries in the region. An estimated $5 billion is being raised in infrastructure investment funds that will be seeking equity interests in such projects, usually arranging additional debt finance as well. Many of the projects are planned with an exit point for the initial investors, usually equity sales in local or foreign markets.[11] This "expectation," or "plan," assumes that the markets will be able to absorb the issues and that the country will be able to absorb the eventual foreign exchange outflow. Since infrastructure projects rarely earn foreign exchange directly, countries will have to ensure that export growth continues to permit repatriation of dividends and, eventually, principal. The infrastructure supported by these investments may well contribute to enhanced export earnings. Most have been for power generation, with toll roads a distant second.

Other Factors Affecting Capital Flows

Credit Ratings

Commercial bank lenders and direct investors are presumed to have direct country knowledge on which to base their investment decisions. Even these investors, however, cannot always know the country intimately or be sure they are protected from adverse factors beyond the immediate concerns of the project. Association with local partners is often sought to gain vital local knowledge. (It is also sometimes required by the recipient country, although such restrictions are declining in East Asia.) Beyond whatever assurances direct investigation and local partners can bring, foreign investors will be influenced by the general reputation and credibility of the country receiving the investment and by the stability of the macroeconomic policy environment. Banks and other investors have learned, to their loss, that policy weaknesses can have adverse effects on even the best projects and sovereign loans.

Indirect investors typically have less involvement in a country and tend to rely more on intermediate sources of information—for example, credit ratings both for the country and for an individual issue. Some institutional investors are constrained by their own regulatory authorities to invest only in securities that have a formal credit rating above a specified category. Thus the higher the credit

Almost all borrowers in East Asia are investment grade.

TABLE 2.15 CREDIT RATINGS OF SELECTED EAST ASIAN SOVEREIGN BORROWERS,
MARCH 1995
(percentage of GDI)

Economy	*Moody's rating*	*Standard and Poor's rating*
Singapore	Aa2	AA+
Taiwan (China)	Aa3	AA+
Korea, Rep. of	A1	A+
Thailand	A2	A–
Malaysia	A2	A
Hong Kong	A3	A
China	A3	BBB
Indonesia	Baa3	BBB
Philippines	Ba3	BB–

Note: Countries are ranked in descending order according to ratings by Standard and Poor's and Moody's
Investor Service. The ratings are ranked from highest to lowest as follows:

	Moody's rating	*Standard and Poor's rating*
Investment grade	Aaa, Aa, A, Baa	AAA, AA+, AA, AA–, A+
Noninvestment grade	Ba, B	BB+, BB, BB–, B+, B, B–
Default grade	Caa, Ca, C, D	CCC+, CCC, CCC–, CC, C

In addition, numbers from 1 (highest) to 3 are often attached to differentiate borrowers within a given grade.

Source: Financial Times; International Financing Review; and Solomon Brothers.

rating, the larger the potential market for an issue. Good credit ratings by internationally recognized rating agencies are increasingly important in supporting investor decisions to move into a particular country. Typically, these ratings apply
to issues traded internationally and to a country's sovereign borrowing abroad.[12]
Standardized domestic credit ratings are also important for the development of
national securities markets, and several countries are creating reputable rating
capacity for their own issues. (Malaysia and Thailand have already established
rating agencies; others are planning them.) These ratings will help both national
and foreign investors participate in domestic securities markets with greater comfort. Beyond the formal rating, investors often look to reports or actions of
multilateral institutions and reputable research institutions for information on a
country's prospective overall performance.

Table 2.15 shows East Asian economies that have earned high marks on
international credit ratings. Most economies in the region have attained investment-grade ratings for sovereign issues, and some rank as well as or better
than some industrial countries. These rankings are further evidence of the
economies' integration into world capital markets.

Nationality of Funds

Although we commonly speak of the foreign investor, the nationality of the owner of the capital is no longer a critical factor in determining the "foreignness" of an investment; rather, the currency of domicile of the capital is. A national who brings foreign exchange from an offshore account (directly or through an intermediary) is no different in terms of external capital flows from a foreign investor.[13] It has been estimated that a large part of the external capital flows out of and back into Latin America has been "flight capital" owned by nationals. A recent IMF study (IMF 1995a) concludes that the 1994 Mexican crisis was precipitated by nationals converting their holdings to dollars. (Nonnational investors acted later, after the flight from the peso was well under way.) Flight capital appears to have been less of a problem in East Asia (box 2.4). This is true for both FDI and FPI. Nevertheless, to the extent that capital accounts are open or porous, domestic currency assets can turn into foreign capital, either for flight or to benefit from advantages accorded foreign investment.

Table 2.6 identified the sources of FDI investment in East Asia. (The data only indicate the proximate source of the investment, not its ultimate nationality.) The origins of FPI are more difficult to determine. It is broadly assumed that a large part of it comes from institutional investors in the United States and the United Kingdom—the most active organization and marketing of mutual and emerging market funds occur in these countries, and their institutional investors have the greatest freedom and propensity to invest internationally. The investment horizons of investors in Japan and continental Europe tend to be less global. However, many Asia-oriented funds are managed out of Hong Kong, which shows up in recorded flows as a major source of funds. Furthermore, there is no way of determining the nationality of the investors in these funds. For all intents and purposes, the funds are global capital.

Sustainability

Private capital flows to countries with sound policies and growth potential are likely to be sustainable. (The overall rate of growth slackened in 1994, but this can be explained by cyclical factors.) The variety of sources, the private-to-private structure, and the diversity of instruments all indicate that in the aggregate these flows are more sustainable than the commercial bank borrowing of the 1970s and early 1980s. Several reasons lend confidence to this belief. First and most important, policy reforms and sound macroeconomic environments in recipient countries, coupled with high real growth rates, make these markets highly attractive to investors in terms of risk-adjusted yields. This was true even in the

BOX 2.4   CAPITAL FLIGHT

The issue of capital flight has traditionally been important in Latin America and seems to have contributed to the latest series of devaluations in Mexico. The amounts of these uncontrolled capital flows are difficult to estimate, but a rather substantial errors and omissions entry in the annual balance of payments gives an idea of how large these flows can be.

It has been estimated that the total stock of capital owned by Latin Americans outside the Southern Hemisphere reached between $210 billion and $250 billion in 1991, up by more than $100 billion from 1984. In Mexico alone the estimated increase between the mid-1980s and the early 1990s was over $40 billion—twice the official foreign exchange reserves held by that country in early 1994.

In Asia estimates of capital flight are harder to come by, mainly because those capital flows have not played such havoc with economic policy and exchange rates there.

Nevertheless, Philippine economists have estimated that of every $100 that come in, $25 go out in capital flight. In Thailand the errors and omissions category averaged over $700 million in unaccounted capital flows between 1987 and 1991 and $430 million in unaccounted outflows during 1992–93. The Indonesian errors and omissions were more serious, with outflows averaging nearly $1.5 billion for all but two years between 1987 and 1993. China and Malaysia have also experienced large outflows in the errors and omissions account, but much of this has apparently been reinvested in the country to benefit from special treatment accorded "foreign" investment (see box 2.1).

The relative openness of capital accounts in East Asia and the close working relations among financiers in most countries offer a large potential for substantial amounts of capital flight; hence the importance of maintaining sound policy. These countries avoided serious capital flight after the Mexico crisis, although the threat was real.

1980s for most of East Asia, which accounts for the continued strength of flows into the region. A recent survey of Japanese companies by the Export-Import Bank of Japan revealed that seven of the ten countries judged most promising for long-term FDI lie in East Asia. Second, the liberalization of capital transactions in both recipient and source markets has lowered transaction costs and risks, facilitating international investment. Third, developing countries represent a very small portion of assets in global portfolios and much less than standard portfolio diversification theory would suggest. It is estimated that institutional portfolios in the United States alone amount to $9 trillion, of which $2.6 trillion is in stocks. Only 10 percent is invested abroad, and less than 1 percent is in emerging markets. It has been suggested, on the basis of a model of weighted proportional representation of global assets, that an optimized global portfolio would have perhaps 4 to

5 percent of its assets in quality emerging market issues. Thus the scope for expansion is large.

Recent analysis in portfolio management theory and experiences with various high-yield, high-risk assets have demonstrated that diversifying into assets in markets not fully integrated with the markets in which most of the portfolios are invested can raise returns more than risks.[14] Research has confirmed the weak integration of most emerging markets with industrial country markets. High returns in developing countries, combined with the decline in returns on assets in industrial countries, have made investments in these markets relatively more attractive, despite higher risks. As such flows become easier for both regulatory and technical reasons, the basic economics are overwhelmingly in their favor. Sophisticated asset valuation models are also used to help determine fundamental values and to identify market-pricing anomalies that offer potential short-term gains. Gains related to short-term exchange rate and interest rate movements or new stock issues are sought, and market expectations play a large role in portfolio investment decisions. Hence, there is a substantial speculative undertone to some of these investments.[15]

A simpler view might be based on a straightforward stock adjustment process, which indicates that the recent expansion of investment flows could continue for some time—until the share of emerging market issues in portfolios is closer to the theoretical equilibrium level. The existence of large mutual funds and pension funds in industrial countries, particularly the United States and the United Kingdom, enhances this process of portfolio diversification. These institutional investors aggregate large volumes of funds from small savers and add them to the pool of professionally managed global capital. The larger pools are better positioned to diversify risks along the lines suggested above. However, we have no way of estimating the time path or rate of adjustment of portfolios to include more international and emerging market assets, and no assurance that the stock adjustment will be smooth or will affect all countries similarly. The basic trend of the adjustment may be relatively slow, since research indicates a strong home-country bias in most portfolios, despite theoretical models urging international diversification. This trend may be a benefit because market capitalization in East Asia or Latin America is small relative to potential external capital movements, and small portfolio reallocations could have large impacts on individual markets.

Reversibility and Volatility

On top of the fundamental trend of expanding capital flows into emerging markets, one can also expect substantial volatility in short-term prices and volumes, which encourages speculation. Volatility is more likely to be a short-term problem in specific countries at specific times, when there is uncertainty or speculation. By itself, volatility does not entail a shift in underlying trends, although increases in volatility may foreshadow more fundamental changes in market views. Reversals are more discrete changes in trends and may occur, as just happened in Mexico, in response to shocks that change expectations. In aggregate, the flows are likely to be more stable because of the strength of underlying forces supporting greater internationalization of capital markets, as discussed above. Nevertheless, the flows are likely to vary over time as a function of many factors in international and industrial country markets, as well as local factors. The potential variability of flows will have to figure in the decision matrices of authorities in recipient countries.

It is in the nature of private portfolio flows to be extremely sensitive to factors that affect yield, and changes in expected yields may lead to changes or reversals in trends. Part of the recent surge in capital flows occurred because investors sought short-term capital gains as asset prices skyrocketed in emerging markets in 1993. As the increase in values slowed in 1994, so did the flows. Some part of the recent surge is also attributable to the decline in U.S. interest rates over the past two years; the increase in U.S. rates in 1995 led to some reversals. Furthermore, institutional investors are highly sensitive to potential losses or even comparative declines in their own yields, so they may move out of these markets at any early sign of trouble. Because information is imperfect in emerging markets and transaction costs are relatively high, foreign investors may demand a premium to initially enter a market. Once relative yields exceed such a premium, there may be a surge of capital, giving the appearance of herd behavior. The same may be true on the outflow side. In addition, when information is imperfect, the actions of agents who are presumed to be sophisticated lead other agents to react in the same way—a more direct demonstration of herd action.[16] Where expectations are a major factor in investment decisions, it is easy to see that small changes in observed facts can lead to large changes in expectations, and thus to large capital flows.

Risks

Investing abroad has always been perceived as carrying extra risks stemming from, for example, different procedures, different legal structures, and sovereign interventions. No simple measure exists to indicate whether overall risk has been increasing or decreasing over time, but price fluctuations indicate greater variability in recent years. Despite vast increases in the availability of information and the speed of its transmission and processing, risks for international flows remain high. The increased use of floating or variable exchange rates in most countries; the large swings in interest rates in major commercial countries; and systemic stresses—brought on by the oil crises, the fall of the Eastern bloc, a lack of policy coordination among industrial countries, and national and international financial sector crises—have all contributed to uncertainty and volatility in international financial markets. These risks are faced in varying degrees by lenders and borrowers alike.[17] The risk factors imply that investors are going to require higher rates of return to place funds internationally, especially when investing in another currency, and that risk management tools will become more important in these transactions.

Spreads on loans and bonds to developing countries are typically above comparable rates for most industrial countries, depending on the instrument, borrower, and time period.[18] But these loans and bonds represent a small portion of total flows. Rates of return on FDI and equity are generally considered quite high—hence, the large flows. Target rates of return above 30 percent are often mentioned. Although actual data are scarce, actual returns of over 25 percent per year have been reported by U.S. FDI investors. Yields on equity investments (including appreciation) were very high in 1993 but slumped in early 1994. Partial evidence from early negotiations for BOOT infrastructure investment indicates that high rates demanded by private investors have slowed the conclusion of a number of project agreements.

Countries opening their financial markets, as well as international investors, are taking steps to reduce or manage the risks involved. Management of risk is important because private investors are very sensitive to risk factors. Two elements of risk management need to be considered: absolute reduction in risk and reallocation of remaining risk to the agents best able to deal with it. Absolute risk can be reduced by matching assets and liabilities, by stabilizing economic management, by ensuring predictable and orderly markets, by increasing information and reducing uncertainty, and so on. Many of these factors can be influenced by government policy, and reducing the risks they pose investors should be a major government objective.

To better deal with the remaining risks inherent in uncertain investment decisions, capital markets have developed a number of financial instruments to spread risks, insure against a variety of adverse outcomes, and otherwise protect participants in uncertain markets, both domestic and international. These instruments come under the general headings of derivatives and hedges and can take on a bewildering variety of forms, of which futures, forwards, and options are the most common. Where derivatives markets exist, developing countries as well as investors can use these instruments, but in fact, most of these markets are in major financial centers and deal in instruments denominated in major currencies. Thus derivatives and hedges are of limited usefulness in emerging markets. As developing country markets grow, however, they are adding derivatives to their offerings. The largest derivatives market in a developing country is in Brazil, where it helps deal with the uncertainties of currency fluctuations. Hong Kong and Singapore are also developing active markets in some forms of derivatives.

Derivatives require large and active underlying markets and complex investors on both sides. They have their own costs, and their availability is differentiated in large part on the basis of a participant's creditworthiness. Recent experiences have shown that derivatives can be misused and can lead to large losses, so care must be exercised when dealing in these complex instruments. An extensive literature on the use and risks of derivatives exists; further discussion is beyond the scope of this paper.

Notes

1. This discussion is based on the source of the funds, public (official) or private. A number of private-source funds receive government guarantees in the recipient country and are thus counted as official in the *World Debt Tables* (World Bank 1996). However, the value of government guarantees has considerably diminished since the debt crisis, and in terms of lenders' decisionmaking it is more useful for our purposes to consider the sources. In addition, private lenders sometimes seek guarantees (full or partial) from their own governments or from multilateral agencies.

2. The high volume of foreign private capital that moved into Latin America around 1980 (the only other period of sustained high private flows into the region) was largely in the form of syndicated loans and frequently did not increase productive investment. Rather, it led to the debt crisis.

3. FDI flows can either increase investment or fill an ex ante current account deficit, but not both. In the latter case they also validate lower domestic saving, which may not be desirable, particularly if the capital inflow is not likely to be sustainable.

4. Because the funding base was initially the Eurodollar market, which was beyond the control of national monetary authorities, Eurodollar and, later, Eurocurrency lending was possible despite capital controls in many industrial countries. With the demise of those controls, the funding base of these loans is potentially larger, and the primary limit on volume comes from the lenders' prudential decisions.

5. The disputes center on whether the central government is responsible for repayment defaults by local governments and state-owned enterprises that did not obtain an explicit guarantee from the central government. Lenders argue there was an implicit guarantee, which the government denies.

6. In general, investment, whether in export-oriented or in import-substituting activities, is beneficial in a nondistorted economy. However, in the presence of distortions favoring import substitution, investment in those activities may have fewer or even negative welfare effects, despite profits earned by the activities themselves.

7. Over the past decade Malaysia has privatized more than $4 billion in assets. However, the bulk of these assets has been transferred to national investors as part of a

program to diversify ownership of capital. The Philippines undertook privatization in large part to undo the public accumulation of commercial enterprises resulting from bailouts of insolvent firms during the Marcos regime. These firms were sold as part of the resolution of the debt crisis.

8. Some analysts (see Kim and Singal 1993) assert that opening domestic capital markets leads to a decline in volatility after about a year; others disagree (Howell 1993).

9. Some governments (such as those of Indonesia, Korea, and Thailand) have been able to place bonds in industrial country markets for over a decade and have investment-grade ratings. Private borrowers' access to these markets is a more recent phenomenon.

10. Note that the global debt crisis prior to the one in the 1980s involved Latin American bonds placed in U.S. and U.K. markets in the 1920s and early 1930s, which were defaulted. This experience led to the use of bank lending, to no better avail. Now bonds are once again viewed as a desirable vehicle for lending to developing countries, in part because they were serviced during the bank debt crisis of the 1980s.

11. These funds are typically structured to raise substantial capital to be invested in a series of infrastructure projects. The fund would take some combination of equity and debt, with a strong preference for the former. Other financing would be obtained, and technical and local partners would be involved. The fund would expect to earn dividends for a number of years, sell the equity to complete a cycle, and return the expected large investment yields to the initial investors. Sale of the equity would occur on national markets (to national or foreign investors) and perhaps abroad, depending on the enterprise. This structure depends on the development of national capital markets and on their being continuously attractive to investors worldwide.

12. Typically a country is rated for sovereign risk on specific issues, and companies within a country may also be rated. Firms are usually rated no higher than the country because of the issue of sovereign risk. Rare exceptions occur when firms have independent access to foreign exchange to service the security.

13. Where exchange regulations would force a national to convert foreign exchange on entry or otherwise treat the national differently from a nonnational, it is likely the national would act through a nonnational intermediary, such as a shell corporation located in a tax haven.

14. Basically, if markets were fully integrated, rates of return movements would be highly correlated, and the benefits of diversification into these markets would derive from the spreading of risks across a wider variety of assets and from the fundamental differences in growth rates among the various economies. In theory these differentials would be offset by exchange rate movements, but in practice the short-to-medium-term fluctuations in exchange rates do not reflect the fundamentals. Diversification among integrated markets proves to be good strategy. When markets are not fully integrated, their price movements are not highly correlated, and diversification into poorly integrated markets offers greater risk protection. If the nonintegrated markets also have high yields, this investment can considerably strengthen a portfolio.

15. The recovery of Latin American debt values and the subsequent rapid growth of share values in those heretofore depressed markets created many profit opportunities that risk-tolerant investors are seeking to replicate in other emerging markets.

16. This was clearly evident in the surges of syndicated bank lending before and during the debt crisis. The reactions following the Mexican devaluation in December 1994 further demonstrate the power of herd behavior. Many institutional portfolio managers bailed out so that they would not have to explain why they held Mexican paper. (See the article by Robert McGough and Sara Caliam, *Wall Street Journal*, January 13, 1995, p. 1.)

17. In particular, there is growing concern that movements in exchange rates are poorly correlated with long-term economic fundamentals. This is worrisome for those who believe the exchange rate is critical for proper allocation of resources internationally. Consideration is being given to ways of reducing such volatility on a global basis.

18. In some cases, however, a strong developing country is perceived to be as good as or better than some of the weaker borrowers in industrial countries.

Country Experience in East Asia

Expanding investor interest and capital inflows have affected nearly all countries in East Asia, posing dilemmas for policymakers. The issues are more pronounced now than a couple of decades ago because of the greater degree of interdependence with the rest of the world and the greater scrutiny given countries' actions and policies by official bodies (such as the WTO) and by the private sector. (Countries that launched rapid, export-oriented growth in the 1960s and 1970s faced a simpler world and less scrutiny.) East Asian countries have responded positively to the increased capital flows, generally by liberalizing capital markets, facilitating foreign investment, and easing ownership restrictions. Countries' situations have varied, and so have specific reactions, in accordance with circumstances and policy objectives. Most countries have experienced pressures for currency appreciation, growing reserves, and volatility of capital flows. As with trade and macroeconomic policy, the financial sector policy response is being handled pragmatically; crises have been managed or avoided, and the results are heartening (see Corbo and Hernández 1994 for a comparison of experiences in Latin America and East Asia).

Key Issues in East Asian Countries

East Asian countries have achieved high growth rates through market-based development and export orientation. Basic macroeconomic stability has been a key element in this success, but, like many other developing country governments, those in East Asia have used policy interventions and incentives to aid growth. They have been cautious as to how and when they have opened their economies. Interventions have included, to varying degrees, repression in the financial sector, allocated credit, managed exchange rate policies, and a variety of controls on foreign capital. In most cases the distortions have been mild, and maintenance of low inflation and high growth has helped avoid some of the worst problems associated with more extreme forms of intervention. Governments have encouraged exports to promote efficiency and have generally forced economic agents to meet market tests in order to merit government support. The scope, extent, and type of policy intervention have differed from country to country. There has been considerable debate as to whether interventionist policies contributed significantly to the observed high rates of growth. (See, for example, World Bank 1993a for further discussion of the pros and cons of financial repression and other interventions in East Asia.) That debate will not be pursued here; whatever degree of intervention might have occurred, it has not prevented these economies from growing rapidly.

Monetary policy and financial sector incentives have been used to promote development, moderate domestic demand, and, on occasion, protect the capital account and reserves. Countries were able to isolate many of these policies from external forces by means of the structure of capital controls and, until recently, because international capital was relatively uninterested in these markets and had difficulty moving into them. Interest rate controls have reduced costs to selected producers, and exchange rate policies, usually gradual depreciation, have helped exporters. Governments have been seen as standing ready to cushion financial markets against losses through a variety of measures that have amounted to implicit or explicit guarantees not fully priced to the recipients.[1] In many cases, implicit guarantees or governments' credit allocation policies have contributed to poor decisions in the financial sector, which is still fragile in many East Asian countries.

Reform programs are gradually reducing direct controls and opening capital accounts and capital markets to greater foreign participation. Market responses to these reforms have highlighted the weakness of some of these markets and have led to further reform and more liberal market environments. Important consequences of greater integration into global capital markets have been changes in the options for managing macroeconomic policy and a more circumscribed scope for direct intervention by the authorities. International factors now play a larger role in determining options for national policy, and governments need to take a much broader view of economic forces in formulating and executing policy. The more open the economy, the larger the potential economic gains but, also, the more complex the policy framework for achieving stability and sustained high growth. Increasingly, economies have little choice but to open up more in order to sustain rapid growth.

Countries in the region represent a wide variety of income levels and economic experiences—factors that affect their implementation capacity and objectives in managing capital flows. This diversity is not amenable to a linear taxonomy of, for example, income-based stages for policy reforms, as the country experiences presented in the next section demonstrate. There are, however, broad typologies that may be useful to policymakers.

Transitional versus market economies. The most important distinction is between economies in transition and those that have long had market-based economic systems. In the former, establishing clear rules on property rights, asset transactions, and capital markets is of paramount importance in facilitating capital flows. This has to be coordinated with appropriate modification of policy instruments so as to move away from direct controls and credit allocation. China demonstrates that credible commitment to reform is as important as completion of the reform process; it has been able to attract substantial amounts of foreign investment, primarily FDI, while the reform process is still in progress. The shift to a market-based system implies not the absence of government action but, rather, a shift from government intervention in direct allocative decisions to the establishment and enforcement of a set of rules which encourages private agents to make efficient allocative decisions and ensures that commitments can be carried out. These concerns also apply to other countries, although less acutely.

Low- versus middle-income economies. Income level, partly as a proxy for institutional development, suggests differentiation in the kinds of flows countries should expect. It would be reasonable for low-income countries to concentrate more on attracting FDI because of the ancillary benefits it brings in terms of management skills, technology, and access to markets. FDI poses less of a macromanagement challenge to governments whose administrative capacity may be weak, and it does not require as developed a financial market structure. Since low-income countries are less likely to have the kind of liquid wealth needed to support an active capital market, this emphasis would be consistent with their own economic capabilities. As countries grow and accumulate more assets, the natural pressures to expand the base for private resource mobilization and for investment in intangible assets will support an expansion of domestic capital markets, which will facilitate accommodation of more portfolio investment. It is also likely that over this period macroeconomic management will have become more sophisticated and better able to deal with the impact of such flows on domestic aggregates. Quite clearly, only after relatively broad and deep markets have been established in the fundamental instruments can a country move on to more sophisticated instruments, as a few of the most advanced countries in the region are now doing.

East Asian economies, regardless of income level, have demonstrated rapid learning curves in economic management as new challenges have presented themselves. Perhaps the most important element in their success has been their commitment to a stable macroeconomic environment. Most have also shown a strong preference for encouraging FDI. However, the range of models is broad. China, Korea, and Taiwan (China) discouraged foreign investment for much of their early growth and relied more on foreign borrowing than many countries would now find comfortable. Indonesia opened its capital account at a very early stage and learned to manage monetary policy in that situation. Others have been more open to FDI from relatively early stages in their development.

Fundamental to the success of the East Asian economies has been exceptional performance on both investment and domestic saving. These countries have managed to invest very large shares of GDP productively. The high level of investment alone explains a great deal of their growth and distinguishes the region from most of the rest of the developing world. Perhaps as impressive is that these high rates of investment have been sustained over many years. As figure 3.1 shows, the share of investment is currently well above 30 percent in most of the region. (Indonesia's is slightly below that, and the Philippines is lagging as it struggles with its reform program.) Table 2.2 has shown that foreign capital has been an important component of this investment, particularly in recent years, and has undoubtedly contributed more than just financial resources. Ready availability of foreign capital is one explanation for the steady increase in investment rates over the past three decades, as shown in figure 3.1.

East Asia's high investment rates have been supported by consistently high domestic saving rates, but explaining the factors that have contributed to this

East Asian countries have steadily increased their investment rates.

FIGURE 3.1   INVESTMENT AS A SHARE OF GDP, EAST ASIA, 1970–94

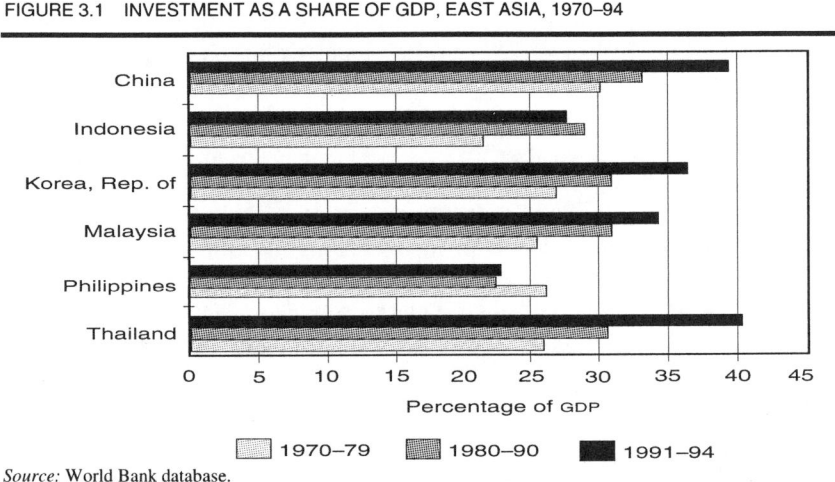

Source: World Bank database.

Most important, domestic savings has also risen in East Asia.

FIGURE 3.2   SAVINGS AS A SHARE OF GDP, EAST ASIA, 1970–94

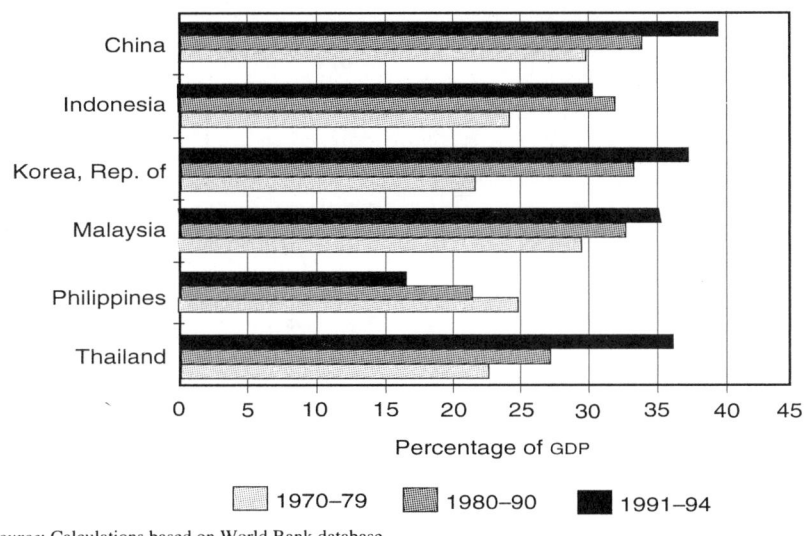

Percentage of GDP

☐ 1970–79   ▨ 1980–90   ■ 1991–94

Source: Calculations based on World Bank database.

high and sustained saving behavior is not easy. In an important sense, the high rates of domestic saving mean that these economies are less dependent on foreign saving to finance their high investment rates and thus are less vulnerable to swings in foreign capital flows. By contrast, in Latin America, where saving rates have typically been much lower, swings in the availability of foreign capital have had much larger effects on investment and growth rates. (See box 3.1 for an analysis of the Mexican crisis.) This situation has led to a series of boom-and-bust cycles that follow the ebb and flow of foreign capital—something East Asia has largely avoided. In fact, as noted in chapter 2, recent capital flows to East Asia have exceeded the gaps between domestic saving and investment and have contributed to a buildup in reserves.

Remarkably, even with the surge in capital inflows in the 1990s, East Asian economies have been able to sustain or even increase already high domestic saving (figure 3.2). The Philippines is the lone exception, and its recent reform measures give hope that it, too, will get its saving performance up to the norms of the rest of the region. The combination of high investment and high domestic saving is a primary source of strength for these economies and facilitates the absorption and management of substantial capital flows.

Looking forward, all these countries will have large capital requirements, both for directly productive investment and for economic infrastructure, if they are to

BOX 3.1   THE RECENT CURRENCY CRISIS
IN MEXICO

Since 1990 Mexico has experienced:

- A steady and substantial real appreciation of its exchange rate
- A large current account deficit (over $23 billion a year, or 7 percent of GDP, since 1992)
- An even larger inflow of external capital ($25 billion to $30 billion a year since 1992)
- A decline of the domestic private saving rate
- Stagnant domestic investment and productivity.

As part of a program to bring inflation down, the Mexican government maintained its exchange rate within a narrow band as a nominal anchor and relied on a high rate of capital inflows to sustain the current account deficit. Inflation dropped from 159 percent in 1987 to 8 percent in 1994. However, a large proportion of the flows ended up in increased consumption; fixed investment remained at about 21–22 percent during 1987–93. This left the economy vulnerable to the pace of foreign capital inflows. When net capital inflows declined from $31 billion in 1993 to about $10 billion in 1994, reserves fell sharply, from $25.4 billion at the end of 1993 to $6.5 billion as of December 21.

What Happened?

Mexico tried to defend an overvalued exchange rate for too long. When the government devalued the new peso by 15.3 percent on December 20, 1994, investors read this as a major break in policy, and their confidence in the economy was severely shaken. Domestic investors acted first, shifting their holdings to U.S. dollars and depleting official reserves. Capital outflows became intense as investors tried to protect their positions. On December 22, with the reserves nearly depleted, the government announced that the Mexican peso would float. As the situation became clearly unsustainable, foreign investors fled the market, and

sustain their high growth rates. The traditional resources for infrastructure—government savings and foreign official borrowing—are not likely to be sufficient to meet the demand for infrastructure investment, estimated at $1.5 trillion over the next ten years. Private sources of finance will be required to augment public sources, and foreign investment is expected to be a large component of that financing. Maintaining or augmenting foreign flows and directing them into productive investment are important policy objectives for these countries.

Before turning in more detail to the policy and regulatory issues related to managing external capital flows, we present a brief synopsis of recent experiences of some East Asian countries in dealing with external capital flows. (For a fuller discussion of country experiences, the reader should consult the relevant references.)

confidence in the Mexican economy was undermined.

The Mexican government has since begun implementing a stabilization program that focuses on restraining wages, reducing fiscal spending, tightening monetary policy, and accelerating structural reform. The U.S. government has provided an emergency support package of more than $20 billion, with further support from the IMF ($17.8 billion) and others.

The Lessons

■ Exchange rates should be flexible and should be combined with appropriate monetary and fiscal policy so that the current account deficit does not grow to unsustainable levels. Use of the exchange rate as a nominal anchor to restrain inflation cannot be pursued for too long.

■ Monetary policy may not be adequate by itself. In the Mexican case, high interest rates helped attract short-term capital. More restraint on quasi-fiscal expenditure was needed. Foreign capital inflows were not able to support an overvalued currency for long.

■ Using foreign capital inflows to finance consumption is not sustainable. Capital inflows should be directed into investment, to increase productivity and repayment capacity.

■ Foreign savings should not be allowed to substitute for domestic savings. In Mexico domestic saving as a percentage of GDP has declined from 19 percent in 1990 to less than 15 percent in 1994.

■ Foreign portfolio flows are more volatile than FDI and are thus more likely to be pulled out when a country's macroeconomic condition deteriorates. Between 1990 and 1994 portfolio flows in Mexico dominated (at 47 percent of total inflows), compared with 8.7 percent for China, 16 percent for Indonesia, 23 percent for Malaysia, and 27 percent for Thailand.

■ Issuing bonds denominated in or linked to foreign exchange (the Tesobonos) is very risky and poses a real threat to reserves, especially when investor confidence is weak.

Country Experiences

China's capital market has been developing rapidly, starting from essentially nothing, as the country has embarked on rapid market reforms. China's integration into the international capital market has attempted to follow orderly, natural, and sequential steps: official borrowing first, private FDI second, and private portfolio investment last. But its markets are still fragmented, and the development of these markets is far from complete.

As it opened its trade regime and product markets, the Chinese government entered the international capital market through commercial bank borrowing and issuing of international bonds in the late 1970s. Official borrowing totaled $10.6 billion during 1979–82 and continued to increase throughout the 1980s. In the first stage of domestic capital market development (1981–90), government bonds and corporation stocks were issued only to domestic investors. These instruments were issued essentially to mobilize savings and were held rather than traded. Although the total amount of securities issued reached over 175 billion yuan by the end of 1990, a formal secondary market could not develop because an adequate legal framework and institutional infrastructure were lacking. In the real sector, however, the investment climate was greatly improved. Government at all levels attempted to attract FDI through favorable tax concessions and tariff exemptions and by creating various special economic development zones with more flexible policies toward FDI. Inflows of FDI, most of which was in the form of joint ventures, increased gradually, from $0.6 billion in 1983 to $4.4 billion in 1991, and then rose dramatically, reaching $27.5 billion in 1993 and more than $33 billion in 1994 (see table 2.5 and box 2.1).

As a result of the rapid growth of the informal equity market, the gradual building of a legal and institutional infrastructure, and increased openness to foreign investments, China was able to open two securities exchanges in 1990 and 1991. This marked the beginning of a real capital market there. In 1993 nationwide regulations on stock issuance and exchanges went into effect, and a national regulatory body, the China Securities Regulatory Commission, was established. To attract foreign portfolio investors under a nonconvertible currency system, the Shanghai and Shenzhen exchanges started to list "B" shares in 1992, beginning China's integration into world capital markets. The B shares were denominated in renminbi yuan, traded in China, and open exclusively to foreign ownership. ("A" shares were open only to Chinese nationals.) By December 1994, of the 291 companies that listed A shares for domestic investors, over 40 also listed B shares for foreign investors. The Chinese government encourages healthy domestic companies to list on overseas exchanges through ADRs and GDRs.[2]

China's equity market is still segmented, with A shares designated for citizens and B shares for foreigners. In time this segmentation should be eliminated, as the Chinese currency is expected to become convertible by 1998. Meanwhile, the government has intervened to regulate the rate of new issues in both markets and the extent of foreign participation, partly to influence the volume of shares and the effective cost of raising new capital in these markets. The government recently decided to allow domestic pension funds to invest in A shares, adding more demand to the market in order to strengthen its depth and liquidity. Other actions also appear designed to enhance share values in a slumping market. Intervention is perhaps unavoidable at this early stage of market development, but excessive manipulation runs the risk of discouraging stable, long-term investors and creates opportunities for domestic and foreign speculators. In view of China's daunting tasks of restructuring thousands of

SOEs, equity markets should be allowed to expand and play a bigger role in ownership restructuring. The government has recently announced plans to expand the bond market to "wholesale" dealers and institutions, setting the stage for more indirect monetary policy actions.

Indonesia has maintained an open capital account since the 1970s. It, too, repressed the financial sector, although to a diminishing degree. Interest rates were controlled, credit was allocated through the state-owned banking institutions, and preferential rates were accorded to strategic industries. With much of the financial sector in the hands of state enterprises and intermediation spreads high, the open capital account allowed financial intermediation to move offshore for major players, but there was little incentive for portfolio investment to flow in. The open capital account also provided a check on government policies, in that the threat of capital flight prevented domestic disequilibriums from becoming too great. Declining oil revenues, evidence of slowing growth, and persistent exchange rate overvaluation led the government to initiate a broad reform program in the 1980s. In a series of policy packages beginning in 1983, the government undertook substantial reform of the financial sector in conjunction with reforms of trade and investment policy and exchange rate depreciations. Major packages followed in 1988, 1990, 1991, and 1993. Over time, the authorities deregulated interest rates, reduced direct lending by Bank Indonesia, opened the market to greater private (and eventually foreign) bank participation, lifted offshore banking restrictions, and strengthened the regulatory regime. The objective of these policy actions was to lower spreads, improve the efficiency of the financial sector, increase financial deepening, and reduce government dominance. Because of continuing exchange and country risks, real domestic interest rates remained high compared with those of neighboring countries, and the financial sector was still fragile.

The combination of the open capital account, limited open market instruments of monetary policy, and the weakness of government-owned financial institutions constrained the effectiveness of monetary policy and led to occasional reversion to direct controls in the face of undesirable short-term flows. In 1987 and again in 1991 the government required SOEs to convert their time deposits in commercial banks into holdings of Bank Indonesia deposit certificates. This transferred an equivalent amount of foreign exchange to Bank Indonesia, which increased its reserves—in effect, a sterilization. Continuing restrictive monetary and credit policies throughout 1991 and 1992 led to high interest rates and further inflow of foreign capital. Bank Indonesia had to sterilize more than $5 billion, at a substantial cost. In 1989 the government tried to stimulate the economy by lowering interest rates, but the decline in interest rates led to a loss in reserves as short-term funds moved abroad. Monetary policy had to be reversed. An increase in interest rates restored the reserves, and, in an attempt to provide further stimulus, the government lowered reserve requirements from 15 to 2 percent, hoping spreads would fall and credit expand. The move was successful, but deposit rates remained high and continued to draw in capital. Interest rates were again allowed to ease, and more attention was paid to fiscal tightening to rebalance domestic policy. Some reserve losses were tolerated. In mid-1993 Bank Indonesia shifted its open market operations to more flexible, market-determined interest rates and committed itself to minimizing reliance on direct bank reserve transactions in the future. This helped restore confidence in monetary policy and narrow the interest rate spreads between the rupiah and the U.S. dollar and, eventually, between rupiah lending and deposit rates. This more flexible, market-oriented approach to monetary policy proved capable of managing sizable outflows and inflows of foreign capital in 1994.

Throughout this period Indonesia's interest rates have remained high—as much as double its neighbors'—in real terms. It has been argued that this reflects both an exchange premium, traceable to lingering memories of the sharp devaluations of 1978, 1983, and 1986, and a country risk premium, reflecting concerns about the stability and security of the financial system. Econometric analysis has also shown that the offset factor—the amount of monetary creation or contraction that leaks into the foreign sector—is relatively high, at 60 percent (see Hanna 1994b; Das Gupta and Das Gupta 1994). These factors, combined with the open capital account, have considerably reduced Indonesia's ability to pursue an independent monetary policy. If domestic interest rates are to come down, further financial sector reform will be required to increase confidence and reduce the country risk factor. At the same time, continued liberalization, maintenance of low rates of inflation, tight fiscal policy, and steady growth should reduce the exchange risk factor. These measures should bring about a better alignment of Indonesia's interest rates with the international rate, that is, at a lower absolute level. Although financial reform and liberalization have helped saving and investment performance in Indonesia, the openness of the capital account has come at the cost of higher interest rates and constraints on monetary policy. Some argue, however, that these constraints were beneficial in preventing macroeconomic policies from getting out of hand. Indonesia's overall performance has been impressive, particularly in view of the chaotic history of the 1960s.

Korea's financial sector, including its securities markets, was heavily regulated and was closed to foreign investors in the 1970s and early 1980s. The internationalization of Korea's domestic finance and its capital markets started in the mid-1980s. Access to the Korean market by foreign financial institutions was slowly expanded. In 1985 the banking sector was opened to allow foreign banks into the domestic market on an equal footing with domestic banks. In

1987 foreign insurance companies were allowed access to the Korean market. At the same time, international investment trusts were permitted, and foreign and domestic security companies were allowed to do business with each other. This made possible limited foreign ownership of Korean equities through the country funds. The government permitted individual foreign securities companies to own up to 10 percent of the paid-in capital of large domestic securities companies, provided that the total stake of foreign securities companies in a domestic securities company did not exceed 40 percent. Under a guideline announced in November 1990 foreign securities companies were allowed to establish branch offices or joint ventures in Korea.

In parallel, the domestic securities market was expanded by allowing new instruments to be traded, such as convertible bonds in 1985, bonds with warrants in 1987, and depository receipts in 1990. Foreign investment in Korean stocks was permitted in 1992, subject to certain limitations, and substantial overseas capital flowed into the Korean stock market, especially after the fourth quarter of 1992. In 1993 foreigners made net investments of $5.7 billion in the Seoul stock market, bringing the net total investment since the opening of the market in January 1992 to $7.8 billion. By the end of 1993 nearly 9 percent of the shares listed on the exchange were owned by foreigners, accounting for 9.8 percent of total market capitalization. In 1994 the Korean bond market was opened to foreign investors on a limited basis: foreigners were allowed to invest in nonguaranteed bonds of small-scale industries. Since February 1995 Koreans have been allowed to hold foreign currencies without any restrictions, invest up to $300,000 in overseas real estate, and deposit up to $30,000 in overseas banks.

Because of the high growth rate of the money supply and the resulting inflationary pressure by the end of 1993, Korean authorities attempted to slow foreign portfolio investment. When market prices soared, the Korean Stock Market Stabilization Fund sold roughly $500 million of stock. That step proved ineffective, and new rules were announced that required a 20 percent cash deposit in trust accounts, introduced a new foreign investor ID card, and established new stock settlement and proxy standards. The long-term effects of these measures are unclear. The first two should be reconsidered once the perceived crisis has passed.

The integration of the Korean capital market into the global market has been proceeding in an orderly and regulated fashion, with preannounced plans and clearly formulated steps, since 1981. The trend toward more openness is likely to continue, and the government has announced a three-stage program for complete liberalization of financial, capital, and foreign exchange markets by 1998 (see table 3.1). The pace of liberalization, however, has been deliberate and has come late in the development process in comparison with the experiences of other East

Korea drew up detailed plans for its entry into global markets.

TABLE 3.1   BLUEPRINT FOR FINANCIAL LIBERALIZATION AND MARKET OPENING,
KOREA, JUNE 1993

Stage and market	Major items
First stage (1993)	
Financial market	Incrementally introduce the capital adequacy requirements of the Bank for International Settlements
Capital market	Completely liberalize operations of the short-term money market
	Eliminate ceilings on foreigners' stock investment in companies with over 50 percent of equity held by foreigners
	Allow foreign investment trusts and investment consulting firms to participate in the equity of domestic investment trust firms
Foreign exchange market	Expand range of daily interbank foreign exchange rate fluctuations from 0.8 to 1.0 percent
Second stage (1994–95)	
Financial market	Gradually introduce ceilings on aggregate rediscounts
	Diversify short-term financial products (for example, encourage a greater range of maturities for commercial paper)
Capital market	Relax requirements for opening branches of foreign securities firms
	Raise direct stock investment ceilings for foreigners
	Allow international organizations to issue Korean won–denominated bonds in the domestic market
	Permit establishment of domestic representative offices of foreign credit-rating firms
	Raise ceilings on equity participation by foreign investment trust and investment consulting firms
	Completely lift restrictions on overseas portfolio investment for domestic institutional investors
	Raise ceiling on settlement in Korean won for visible transactions
Foreign exchange market	Abolish ceiling on foreign currency deposits exempted from underlying documentation requirements
Third stage (1996–97)	
Financial market	Completely liberalize interest rates, except for demand deposits
	Introduce financial products linked to market rates, such as money market certificates and money market funds
	Gradually lower reserve requirement ratios
Capital market	Permit foreign banks to establish subsidiaries
	Lower capital requirements for branches of foreign securities companies
	Continue to raise direct stock investment ceiling for foreigners
	Progressively permit full settlement in Korean won for visible and invisible transactions
Foreign exchange market	Completely exempt normal transactions from underlying documentation requirements

Source: Cho (1994).

Asian liberalizing economies. Because Korea was able to finance its rapid development with its own high savings and with foreign bank borrowing, and because it often had close technical arrangements with foreign firms for acquiring technology, it had less desire or need to rely on FDI.

Malaysia began deregulating slowly in the 1970s. The pace increased in the 1980s after a major banking sector crisis. Freer capital movements were allowed, some public enterprises were privatized, and trade was liberalized. The economy grew rapidly and was the beneficiary of very large FDI flows, which led to the expansion of a number of export-oriented industries. A boom in exports was followed by increased demand for imports. The current account surpluses generated during 1987–89 gave way to deficits in 1990–93, but because of substantial net capital inflows, reserves shot up. The combination of increased imports, repayment of external debt, reduction of the consolidated government deficit, and tight monetary policy helped maintain low inflation and actually led to a gradual depreciation of the currency through 1991, despite the substantial capital inflows. Subsequently, there has been some mild appreciation. The ringgit has emerged as a strong currency and has attracted the interest of international portfolio investors and speculators as a monetary asset. Malaysia has the largest equity market in East Asia (and the ninth largest in the world), with capitalization more than three times as large as its GDP in 1993.

In late 1993 the government sold ringgit to build its dollar balances at year's end. This led to a temporary depreciation of the currency within its informal trading range. Speculators recognized that the ringgit's fundamentals were very strong and that an appreciation was inevitable, both to recover from the temporary decline due to the government's action and to reflect the currency's increasing strength. They bought ringgit in large amounts, increasing short-term deposits and forward transactions. The government wanted to avoid a sharp appreciation of the currency, and, rather than sell ringgit under what it saw as speculative pressure, it imposed a number of restrictions on capital flows in January 1994. Ceilings were placed on banks' external liabilities, sales of short-term instruments to foreigners were banned, and foreign institutions' ringgit deposits were restricted to non-interest-bearing accounts. These measures stopped the speculation in its tracks. The following month, non-trade-related currency swaps were halted, the sale of private debt of less than one year maturity to foreigners was banned, and maintenance charges were imposed on non-interest-bearing foreign deposits. (Such measures are not unprecedented; Germany and Switzerland took similar actions in the 1960s to stem unwanted capital inflows.)

These actions appeared drastic and led to considerable speculation about capital flight from East Asia. In particular, there was a great deal of concern about future foreign investment in Malaysia after a number of investors suffered losses.

The government made the point that it was not going to be pressured into allowing more appreciation of the currency than it thought appropriate; it was not willing to see speculators make a killing from an exchange rate fluctuation that resulted from government intervention in the market. Once the furor subsided and the exchange rate returned to the level of late 1993, the government gradually removed the controls and freed up capital flows, completely lifting all restrictions by August 1994. The effects of the Mexican crisis in late 1994–early 1995 further reduced pressure on the ringgit, which dipped to near the bottom of its bidding range before recovering by the end of 1995.

In the 1994 incident, drastic short-term measures did forestall speculative pressure on the ringgit when other government actions had left it exposed. Although this decisive reaction restored an equilibrium the government had temporarily disturbed, the government will not be able to buck the market to prevent more fundamental pressures from forcing an eventual appreciation of the currency where growth and long-term inflows remain high and domestic inflation low. The government also learned that its own actions prior to the initial pressure had had consequences. However, over the medium term, upward pressures on the currency are signs of the success of policies for maintaining stability and growth. The authorities properly withdrew once the short-term pressure had passed, and long-term investors retained their confidence in the government's management of the economy.

The *Philippines* was one of the earliest East Asian countries to begin developing its financial markets, partly because of its long-standing association with the United States. Its money market has been active since the 1970s, its stock market was once the largest among developing countries in East Asia, and from an early date foreign banks were permitted to engage in a number of activities. After extensive interest rate liberalization, reform was stalled by the debt crisis of the early 1980s. The Philippines was unable to service its debt, in part because of the country's difficulty in achieving the kind of structural reform put in place by many of its neighbors. The burdens of the debt crisis made further financial sector reform difficult. Net foreign capital flows from private sources essentially ceased for much of the 1980s, and the country had to rely on official assistance. By the end of the 1980s some progress had been made on structural reform. In the early 1990s the debt crisis was resolved, as were a number of structural problems; measures were taken to strengthen the financial sector and restructure two of the dominant financial institutions and a large number of public enterprises.

Once the debt crisis was resolved in 1992 by means of a Brady package with the commercial banks, the country was able to move more quickly on its reform agenda.[3] Growth turned positive and achieved a sustainable 5.1 percent in 1994, which was very satisfactory by Philippine standards, even if somewhat below the growth of other countries in the region. The financial sector was further liberalized, and market-based lending was substituted for a variety of subsidized credits. Four of thirteen universal banks are now foreign owned, representing 9 percent of the banking system's assets. Foreign banks are still limited to three branches, and foreign participation in domestic banks is restricted to 40 percent of the voting stock; this, however, represents a substantial increase in openness compared with the 1980s. In 1995 ten additional foreign banks were permitted to open full-service branches. Decontrol of the foreign exchange market was started in January 1992, when all restrictions on capital repatriation and profit remittances were abolished. In June 1993 the financially distressed central bank was replaced by a more independent Central Monetary Authority, which was then recapitalized. These reforms increased investor confidence in the financial system and the economy, which led in turn to a resurgence of private capital flows.

The domestic money market recovered, and turnover surged to over 100 percent of GDP in 1991. Transactions in the stock market, which had slowed during the debt crisis, recovered to their former level of activity. Foreign investors returned to the Philippines, investing over $3 billion in 1993. More than half of this is portfolio investment—a higher share than in other countries in the region. In 1993 the Manila Composite Stock Index rose 154 percent, marking the best performance among East Asian stock markets for the year. The capital market has played a complementary role in privatization: eighty-one SOEs were sold by February 1994, and many attracted foreign investors.

This influx of portfolio investment, both equity and money market funds, has begun to pose a problem for the authorities. Part of the inflow is short-term capital responding to high domestic interest rates that have been necessary to maintain macroeconomic stability as the country completes its reform program. The government has had to sterilize these flows at some cost to the Central Monetary Authority. In a sense, investor confidence in the foreign exchange regime has been restored more quickly than real adjustments have taken place in the economy. Money is flowing in more rapidly than the economy can absorb it, as indicated by sharp increases in reserves and in the banking sector's foreign liabilities and by the peso's significant appreciation in 1993 and 1994.[4] The government needs to build on its recent reform program to establish the confidence that will encourage investors to move toward longer-term instruments and more FDI.

The Philippines has made significant improvements in the physical and legal infrastructure of the financial system. The Manila Stock Exchange automated its trading system in January 1993, and the Makati Stock Exchange in June. The two stock exchanges have functionally merged through a shared computer system that has eliminated arbitrage trading between the two.

Clearinghouse and depository systems will be computerized and are due to move to paperless trading in 1996. Tougher listing requirements and rules will be implemented to promote fairer allocation of new issues, options and bond trading will be introduced, and a fund to reimburse investors when brokers go bankrupt will be augmented. Assuming that the Philippines' economic recovery continues, the prospects for development of its capital market and its integration with the international market are good.

Thailand, like Malaysia, has long and successful experience in managing large external capital flows. A domestic financial sector crisis in 1983 encouraged the government to hasten its reform of the sector and strengthen its prudential regulations. Oil price increases caused Thailand to experience large current account deficits (unlike Malaysia). Thailand was able to borrow from banks abroad to ride out the crisis, and it took advantage of that cushion during the 1980s to institute wider policy reforms designed to promote exports and increase investment. The reforms worked: growth remained high, and the country's success proved attractive to foreign investors. Thailand has thrived. Substantial current account deficits—as high as 8 percent of GDP—have been recorded every year since 1978 (except in 1986). Although high current account deficits are often a cause for concern, Thailand's deficits have been sustainable because they were associated with a large influx of autonomous foreign direct investment, which was productively invested and which contributed to rapid growth of GDP and exports. The flows were absorbed in higher net imports, relieving pressure on the exchange rate and domestic demand. FDI has accounted for the bulk of capital inflows since the mid-1980s; the flows surged from less than 2 percent of GDP in 1987 to more than 7 percent in 1989 and have remained high since. This led to a jump in investment of more than 10 percent—from 27 to 38 percent of GDP—in the decade ending in 1990. Investment has remained high. The equity market has been deepening, with capitalization over 130 percent of GDP in 1993. In 1993–94 foreign portfolio investment accounted for 27 percent of all capital inflows. The combination of policy reforms and foreign investment brought forth more domestic investment as well.

Thailand's management has been sound. By liberalizing the trade account and allowing larger imports, the country has been able to dissipate the impact of demand from the capital flows. Policies to encourage more investment ensured a rise in growth and export potential. The government initially sterilized a substantial portion of the flows, helped by the strengthened domestic financial sector. It also instituted measures to reduce domestic liquidity, continued financial liberalization, and engaged in a certain amount of moral suasion. As part of the reforms begun in the early 1980s, the government changed its fiscal policies to reduce chronic government deficits, which had contributed to the external deficits of the earlier period. These reforms succeeded in turning the fiscal deficit around and in creating a large surplus. Revenues rose from 16 to 20 percent of GDP, and expenditures declined. Although a great part of the spending cuts fell on current expenditure, investment outlays also dropped by about 1.5 percent of GDP, contributing to an infrastructure deficiency that the country is trying to make up, in part by attracting more foreign investment. This fiscal turnaround helped the country absorb the capital inflows, but at some cost to the domestic economy.

The combination of expanding investment, financial sector reform, active involvement by the Bank of Thailand, and fiscal adjustment has enabled Thailand to avoid most of the negative impacts associated with large-scale capital inflows and to sustain high growth rates. Inflation has been kept under control, the nominal exchange rate has remained stable after a devaluation in the early 1980s, and domestic saving, as well as investment, has remained high. In addition to attracting FDI, Thailand has relied on its domestic banks to raise funds abroad to supplement domestic saving. This has added some risk to that sector (exchange risk, potential short-term capital outflows, and possible conflicts with monetary policy), but the authorities, made wary by earlier financial crises, have carefully monitored these activities. Public investment and other public functions were perhaps cut more than needed and have recently been revived to improve infrastructure and continue poverty programs. Poverty alleviation stagnated around 1990 as modern-sector growth took off, but there are now encouraging signs that poverty is again on the decline. Thailand continues to wrestle with large capital inflows while maintaining overall stability. Consumption is growing faster, but the economy remains attractive to foreign investment. This result is perhaps the best demonstration that, with hard work, national authorities can effectively manage capital flows.

Notes

1. The dangers of such underpriced guarantees are well known and threaten any financial market. The recent savings and loan debacle in the United States is but one example. Historically, financial markets have been able to claim special treatment from the public purse because of the importance of a functioning financial sector to modern economic activity. This special relation is also a basic justification for prudential regulation of financial markets. Problems tend to occur when activities in the market and the extent of regulation are not in balance.

2. A regulation on corporations issuing and listing shares overseas was passed in August 1994. Around sixteen companies have met the requirements for listing "H" shares in the Hong Kong Exchange, and five companies have met those for listing their "N" shares on the New York Stock Exchange. H and N shares may be traded as any other security on those exchanges, often through ADRs in New York.

3. "Brady package" is the common term for a commercial debt-restructuring arrangement whereby earlier, defaulted debt is replaced by new instruments with reduced value but greater security (often provided through collateral). Some debt may also be retired at a discount. Concluding such a deal compensates for outstanding performance deficiencies with creditors and allows the reestablishment of normal financial relations.

4. Pressure has eased following the Mexican crisis. Although there has been some concern that a similar fate could await the Philippines, the fundamental situation is stronger, and a major run on the peso is unlikely.

Issues in Managing Capital Flows in East Asia

Managing large and perhaps variable capital inflows—or, more aptly, managing the economy in such a manner as to effectively and productively absorb these flows—is a major challenge for East Asian countries. Each country has embarked in its own way on a process of liberalizing capital accounts and financial markets, following initiatives in trade liberalization. Until recently, the bulk of capital inflows into East Asia has been FDI and project-related lending, both official and private. At the relatively lower levels of a decade ago, these flows could be readily accommodated. The overall impact of foreign investment on growth and exports has been very positive. As the capital flows have increased, they have created macroeconomic pressures on exchange rates, domestic absorption, investment policies, and the capacities of domestic capital markets. The more recent expansion of portfolio investment implies much more integration into global capital markets and a corresponding increase in exposure to international market discipline—referred to by some as market conditionality—that will circumscribe policy options and limit the range of possible deviation from global norms on a number of variables.

The increased complexity of these flows poses serious policy challenges to authorities, whose primary objective is to promote real sector growth in economies in which the industrial and financial sectors are still rapidly evolving.

Achieving sustainable, rapid growth with open capital accounts and active capital markets may well be more difficult than was true with the more closed financial structures that used to be the norm in East Asia. Indeed, concern about losing control of domestic policy contributed to some governments' reluctance to liberalize their financial sectors and capital accounts in the past, and contributes to their willingness to stop the process if they see it getting out of hand. However, capital controls are becoming more porous, the pressures to liberalize stronger, and the benefits from more open financial sectors more compelling. Government preferences and market forces are converging, and the trend is inevitably toward more liberalization. East Asian countries can continue their rapid growth only if they achieve the efficiency gains that result from further liberalization. Furthermore, less distorted markets provide fewer opportunities for rent-seeking behavior and resource misallocation caused by price and other market distortions.

As capital markets become more open, it is easier for capital, domestic and foreign, to seek the highest rate of return in any market. Investment levels in countries that offer strong growth potential can be augmented by flows of foreign savings. At the same time, sophisticated investors have expanded opportunities to seek short-term gain from exploiting market imperfections, implicit guarantees, and price fluctuations. These latter activities and the extent to which they influence other portfolio investments are more worrisome because of their volatility and their potential impact on long-term policy.[1] They may or may not be responding to fundamentals. Theoretically, speculation and arbitrage are believed to contribute to efficient markets and to impose few net costs overall. Market forces represented by these speculative flows have generally, but not always, created pressures toward needed corrections, either of fundamental policy unbalances or of unwarranted implicit guarantees or distortions.

However, short-term traders can exert a great deal of influence on specific markets at specific times, which can work against government policy objectives. It is argued that short-term traders would do this only if policies were wrongheaded, but in practice market forces make no judgments as to the inherent value of a policy—only as to whether a profit can be made from expected market movements. Market agents have been known to err and overshoot (although policymakers probably anticipate or perceive more errors than are likely to occur). Nevertheless, it is not generally wise policy to try to resist market pressures on the theory that they may be wrong. They are not often wrong, and resistance can be expensive, since today private international markets can mobilize vastly larger sums than even industrial country governments. When market forces do err or overshoot, they correct themselves, usually quickly enough to avoid much lasting harm. In fact, quick policy reaction when the market is applying pressure in response to some perceived profit opportunity often sends a signal that large gains are unlikely and mitigates the flow, whereas digging in against market trends may set up an easy win for speculators at the government's expense. Moreover, where policy failures contribute to market pressures, resistance to adjustment can be very expensive. The burden is on governments to manage their economies so that easy arbitrage opportunities are not readily available and official policies or actions do not give rise to implicit guarantees or other distortions that markets can exploit to the detriment of public objectives.[2] Consistent application of sound policy and clear direction goes a long way toward reducing the likelihood of overreaction by markets. In addition, policymakers can blunt short-term flows that pose dangers to the economy through a variety of instruments that reduce speculative short-term gains.[3]

Governments should naturally exercise caution in opening financial markets to international flows. Liberalization needs to be predicated on (a) developing an appropriate regulatory framework and supervisory system, (b) ensuring that the resulting incentives promote prudent behavior, and (c) adopting a macroeconomic policy structure that is consistent with open financial flows.[4] Policies need to promote both domestic and international equilibrium, be flexible enough to respond to disturbances from the capital markets, and include safety features to activate in periods of crisis. Even with such precautions, the world is a highly uncertain and unpredictable place. There can be no assurances against unforeseen crises, even with the best of policies. This is part of the price of open market economies. The point is not to stifle an economy in order to avoid crises but to ensure that the economy is sufficiently flexible and robust to weather the crises and continue to develop and liberalize despite such interruptions.

Macroeconomic Considerations

The basic theoretical framework for analyzing the impact of external capital flows derives from the pioneering work done by Flemming (1962) and Mundell (1963) on open-economy stabilization policies. Their relatively simple models have been revised (see Marston 1985, on which this section draws) as the issues addressed have become more complex. Policy guidelines have become more complicated and much more dependent on a host of other factors that affect economic activity, including expectations, which can be hard to pin down. The theory provides a useful backdrop and guide for appropriate policy responses, but practical policymaking requires a thorough understanding of the characteristics of the economy in question, the exact nature of the capital flows, and the range of available policy options and tradeoffs. East Asian policymakers have been adept at pursuing reform until difficulties arise, then slowing or even backtracking a bit to reassess and make corrections before moving ahead once more. This pragmatism has proved its worth, as these countries have generally avoided major crises.

The basic theoretical models were initially developed to study the relative effects of monetary and fiscal policies in achieving domestic stabilization. Impacts on the external equilibrium were viewed as results and perhaps as constraints. Critical to the analysis is the exchange regime—fixed or floating—and the openness of the capital account (or the degree of substitutability between domestic and financial capital assets).[5]

Under most conditions, the models indicate that given a fixed nominal exchange rate regime, fiscal policy is relatively more powerful than monetary policy in affecting domestic output. Expansionary fiscal policy increases demand for domestic goods but also tends to raise interest rates as additional public borrowing is required. Higher interest rates attract more foreign capital, increasing reserves. The increase in domestic demand raises the price of nontradables and shifts domestic resources to that sector. The current account balance deteriorates, partly absorbing the increased capital flows. Real currency appreciation occurs as domestic prices rise, even though the nominal rate is fixed.

Conversely, monetary policy has a greater effect on the external account. Raising domestic interest rates attracts foreign capital and builds reserves, the amount depending on the substitutability of foreign and domestic assets. Attempts to stimulate domestic demand by lowering interest rates are diluted, as capital flows overseas to seek higher rates there, reducing any effect on domestic demand. The more substitutable foreign and domestic assets are, the less the interest rate change required for a given effect.[6] Increased substitutability of assets leads to other problems, however. Where governments try to constrain domestic demand by raising interest rates, capital flows in, to benefit from the higher rates, and counteracts the restraint. If sterilization is attempted—if, for example, governments sell bonds (tending to further increase domestic interest rates) to absorb the increase in the money supply associated with the influx of foreign exchange revenues—the inflow of foreign assets could become very large and could overwhelm the authorities' ability to continue to issue bonds to purchase foreign exchange.[7] In such circumstances, it is hard to prevent a real currency appreciation.

For an economy dependent on export growth, as most East Asian countries are, the dangers of expansionary fiscal policy, combined with monetary constraint to keep inflation under control, are evident. East Asian countries generally adopt more conservative fiscal stances than Latin American countries.

Under a floating-rate regime, the additional exchange rate flexibility dampens some of these effects, but at the cost of loss of control over the nominal exchange rate. Fiscal policy becomes relatively less effective in influencing domestic output. The increase in demand from expansion leads to an appreciation of the nominal (and, consequently, the real) exchange rate, increased imports and lower exports, and less demand for money and bonds. Interest rates rise, but less than in the fixed-rate case, and the floating rate keeps the external accounts in balance. The increase in capital inflows offsets the higher current account deficit. Under most reasonable assumptions, output rises, but less than under a fixed exchange rate for a given increase in expenditures. By contrast, monetary policy can have a more compelling effect. An expansionary action, such as open market purchase of domestic bonds, increases output through the effects of money supply on demand. It also leads to a depreciation, which shifts resources to the tradable sector and decreases the current account deficit, offsetting the outflow of capital brought about by the lower interest rate. Reserves remain constant. This scenario holds even with more perfect substitutability of assets, although the interest rate change will be smaller.

These models can also be used in reverse to examine the effects of a change in external variables on the domestic economy. What are the implications when we look at the effect on domestic policy of increases in foreign capital inflows? For a regime with a fixed nominal exchange rate, an increase in foreign inflows tends to reduce the domestic interest rate and increase domestic demand. This, in turn, leads to an increase in domestic prices that will bring about a real appreciation through higher domestic inflation. Reserves tend to accumulate, although by less than the capital inflow, as the current account also deteriorates. Monetary policy action to absorb the capital inflows through, for example, open-market sales of bonds (sterilized intervention) could offset the impact on demand. But such an action would tend to increase interest rates, which could well attract more capital inflow. It is not likely to be effective in the long term if there are practical limits on how many bonds can be issued, and it could be costly (because of negative carry on the reserves accumulated). The more substitutability there is between domestic and foreign assets, the less variance is possible between domestic and foreign interest rates before increases in the domestic interest rate become self-defeating. Fiscal contraction would offset the increase in demand and perhaps allow a reduction in interest rates, which would diminish the attraction of domestic assets to foreign investors. A fiscal response would take longer to orchestrate than a monetary response, however, because public budgets are hard to cut in the short run.

Under a floating-rate regime, a foreign capital inflow leads directly to an appreciation of the nominal and real exchange rates. The impact on output depends on the relative strengths of the increase in demand resulting from the capital inflow and the reduction in demand for domestic output because of the appreciation, but an increase in output is likely. If the exchange rate is allowed to adjust, the real appreciation attributable to the capital inflow has less effect on the domestic economy. Prices may rise, and interest rates may fall. However, for export-oriented economies a sustained appreciation may pose serious long-term problems for the export sector. Many fear that appreciation would cause significant loss of exports and eventually overall growth, as markets are lost to lower-cost competitors.[8] Depending on the relative strengths of different effects, the expansion of domestic demand could be counteracted by either tighter fiscal policy or monetary contraction, offsetting some of the appreciation. The former still raises the same questions about the speed of response; the latter may raise interest rates enough to attract more foreign inflows, exacerbating the initial problem. Furthermore, exchange rate appreciation induced by capital inflows will increase the yield to foreign investors as measured in their own currencies, which may extend the capital inflows, particularly short-term, yield-sensitive flows. The ability of floating exchange rates to insulate an economy from external influences depends on the authorities' willingness to accept exchange rate movements determined, in part, by foreign investment demand. A floating-rate regime also depends on the flexibility of domestic prices and wages and on adequate factor mobility to be effective. The prevailing fixed or managed exchange rate regimes in East Asia and most other countries indicate a marked reluctance to accept the implications of fully floating exchange rates.

Even at this simple level, the models illustrate several important points. The degree of openness of the capital account and the substitutability of foreign and domestic assets have an important bearing not only on financial sector policies but also on real sector policies. Financial flows can have tremendous effects on the real economy—for example, on interest and exchange rates and, through those variables, on output, employment, and trade. The more open an economy and the more integrated into world capital markets, the harder it is for the country to maintain interest rates that deviate significantly from world rates or an exchange rate that is far out of line with what markets believe to be proper.[9] The market's views on these rates are driven by many short- and medium-term considerations and, particularly for interest rates, by forces in the major financial markets. Market pressures on a given country's capital markets reflect a great deal more than just the fundamentals of a particular country. Countries cannot afford to have key policy variables that are inconsistent with global trends. Thus the capital account's openness exposes the economy to pressures that may complicate achievement of the country's long-term real sector objectives, and stabilization issues must be more finely balanced against growth objectives. Integration into capital markets has its price.

To be more realistic in these models, one can admit leakages and other factors—such as unemployed resources, market imperfections, and expectations—that may mitigate or enhance the basic impacts described above. Introducing greater sophistication increases the complexity and number of variables that must be considered in reaching any conclusion, but it does not make reaching a conclusion any easier. In fact, the results can be less determinant. The amount of unemployment in the economy affects the extent to which changes in aggregate demand move output or prices. In developing economies with limited factor mobility among sectors, the question of unemployed resources may have to be considered on a sectoral as well as an aggregate level, or by skill level. Depending on the particular model used, the inclusion of expectation variables introduces an element of guesswork as to what kind of expectation function private investors will apply to any government action or nonaction. In some cases, where governments have announced a commitment to protect exchange rates or fix interest rates, guesswork is reduced for the market, but possibly at the cost of offering private speculative investors a largely covered bet. In other cases it is much harder to predict whether a policy course outlined by a government will be seen as credible. In these matters credibility is itself an important factor in a policy's effectiveness. The history of government commitment and the market's estimation of the resources the government has available to defend a position figure into this equation. Although models provide useful general guidance and help frame the issues, their implementation must be tempered by an analysis of the features of different instruments and by a number of practical considerations.

The basic dilemma stems from the role of the exchange rate (nominal for short-term transactions and real for long-term decisions) in equilibrating both goods and capital markets as they become more open. Heretofore, developing countries in East Asia and elsewhere have been able to use the level and movement of the exchange rate to affect the goods market almost exclusively. East Asian countries have often used nominal depreciations to maintain stable or slightly falling real exchange rates and so promote exports. As capital markets open, capital flows can create pressures to appreciate the real or nominal exchange rate against targets directed toward the goods market. Attempts to maintain a rate satisfactory for the goods market without adjusting other policy instruments can lead to disruptive capital flows. Either the exchange rate target has to be modified, or other policy instruments must be adjusted. Using the exchange rate as a "nominal anchor" to help combat inflation adds to the burden and can be effective only where fiscal and monetary policies are closely coordinated in support of that objective. In countries with less developed financial sectors, the choice and range of instruments are limited.

Microeconomic Considerations

As the theoretical models have become richer and more complex, so have the range and complexity of the instruments available in the financial world. Most of the stabilization models deal with money and simple bonds as assets and include little, if any, explicit analysis of risk—except as the degree of substitutability of domestic and foreign assets may be taken as a partial proxy for differing risk. The models do not look at the differential impacts of different types of capital flows on specific markets. Chapter 2 described some of the variety of assets and instruments involved in the capital flows into East Asia. The range and variety of instruments are even larger in the financial world, and the effects of different types of capital flow can be quite different. Policymakers need to look at the characteristics of the instruments involved in capital movements in both a short-term and a medium-term perspective to help formulate policy. A brief summary of the relevant characteristics of different categories of instruments follows.

Commercial Banks

Commercial bank borrowing provides resources that are essentially untied. Where the capital flow is directly linked to a specific project, its impact will be in the capital goods markets. It will probably have a high import content, which will absorb a portion of the increase in demand from the capital inflow and ease pressure to appreciate the exchange rate or raise domestic prices. However, because these flows are flexible, they can readily be used to finance budget shortfalls of the government or of enterprises, perhaps delaying necessary fundamental adjustment, as often happened leading up to the debt crisis of the 1980s. In that case they increase aggregate demand and are more likely to lead to inflationary pressure and exchange rate appreciation. Because of its fixed term, the stock of this form of capital is not likely to be volatile. However, flows can stop abruptly, leading to economic stresses, particularly where borrowers have come to rely on foreign flows and have allowed domestic savings to decline. Excessive dependence on commercial bank flows can be risky because there are few built-in hedges to protect the borrower against exchange and interest rate fluctuations.[10] Furthermore, repayment schedules are fixed in foreign exchange, and provision must be made to service this debt on schedule, regardless of the state of the economy or of the project financed.

Foreign Direct Investment

Foreign direct investment initially affects the market for real assets through purchases of new capital goods and construction services for plant construction and expansion or, in the case of privatizations and sales of firms to foreign investors, through purchases of existing plant and equipment. Direct investment may even encourage incremental national saving and investment, either from local partners or from bank borrowing. FDI in new plant increases the aggregate demand for investment goods and, often, for imports, almost always of capital goods, and frequently of other goods as well. Higher demand for imports eases the pressure of capital inflow on the domestic economy, reduces reserve accumulation, and relieves pressure on the exchange rate.[11] Most FDI in East Asia has been of this productive type, and its impact has been manageable. When FDI is in a protected industry, as has occurred in some cases, the profits it earns may not come from real (as opposed to accounting) value added. This form of FDI is least beneficial, as it exploits local market imperfections to the advantage of the foreign investor and may not increase domestic value added or wealth measured in world prices. The eventual repatriation of capital and profits could reduce the host's real income and wealth.

FDI attracted by privatization programs is not as likely to result in much new investment. (Depending on the terms of sale, the new owner may be required to undertake a certain amount of new investment or renovate existing equipment.) When an existing domestic asset is sold, there is no direct increase in the capital stock, although the productivity of the existing capital should increase. FDI received is available for whatever purpose the seller chooses, including reducing an external gap, lowering taxes, or sustaining other current expenditures. The effect depends on what the seller (the government, in the case of privatization, or a private agent, in the case of a private asset sale to foreign interests) does with the proceeds: reduce other debt (which might ease pressure in the banking system), invest in another project (which would increase investment, as discussed above), or spend on other goods, primarily consumption (which would increase aggregate demand and perhaps imports, with no increase in output capacity). To the extent that capital inflows support increased imports without a corresponding increase in investment, domestic savings are reduced.

FDI flows are as sustainable as the underlying attractions—stable policies and profitable opportunities. To the extent that an economy's growth depends on a sustained inflow of FDI—for the level of investment, for technology and skill transfer, or for supporting an export strategy—the importance of maintaining those conditions is evident. Although FDI is not readily reversible, sharp drops in new flows can have repercussions if countries depend on it for future export growth. Similarly, to the extent that countries have increased consumption as a result of increased resources derived from the foreign investment, a reduction in those flows will require perhaps difficult adjustments on the consumption front.

No contractual repayments are associated with FDI. Investors expect a return on their investment—generally a higher rate of return than on loans and bonds because of the higher risks and opportunity costs involved. Malaysia, which has been the beneficiary of substantial FDI, has grown rapidly: an estimated one-third of its current account receipts is now claimed by service payments on FDI. When FDI flows are sustained over a long period, foreigners inevitably come to own a substantial portion of the country's capital stock in the sectors that attracted FDI. This prospect is not viewed with as much concern as it once was.[12] FDI is not likely to be volatile: once invested, the real asset is not going to move, although changes in ownership are possible.[13] Eventually, a foreign investor may want to sell to a local partner or divest onto a local stock market, and the host country needs to be prepared for a repatriation of capital. In times of stress, however, investors may well find ways to get their capital out quickly. Many investors set as a target the recouping of their outlays (which are usually less than total project cost) within two or three years, through repatriated profits.

Foreign Portfolio Investment

FPI potentially has a much wider range of effects, depending on the type of instrument and how it is used. It can occur through securities placed in foreign or domestic markets, including short-term funds and demand deposits. (The relation of these two instruments to physical investment may be limited; they may be much more a function of financial variables.) Although many of its impacts can be similar to those of bank loans and FDI, portfolio investment can also have a much greater effect on domestic capital markets and interest rates. Whereas direct investment raises issues of real sector investment regimes, portfolio flows raise issues of financial and capital market regimes and their management. Portfolio investment touches more on issues of disclosure, accounting, and auditing than does direct investment.

When portfolio investment takes the form of an external placement (bond or equity) and the funds are used to finance new investment, the effects are in the real sector, as discussed for FDI. If the funds are used for other purposes, the result depends on those purposes. Paying down debt might ease pressure in the banking sector or build reserves. If the inflow is subsequently invested in domestic capital markets or deposited in banks, the money supply and domestic credit expand. Demand for assets, including real estate, would probably increase, with effects similar to those of foreign investment in local markets (discussed below). If the funds are used for consumption, pressure on domestic output could increase, leading to a rise in prices. These uses are likely to put more upward pressure on the exchange rate and downward pressure on interest rates, as the prices of nontradables and domestic assets are bid up. This is true whether the government or the private sector carries out the initial borrowing or stock issue. Offshore placements do not give rise to volatility concerns in the issuing country's market. Subsequent trading in the asset occurs in the foreign market and does not result in further capital movements, other than normal repayments, into or out of the borrowing country. Sustained access to foreign markets is another matter; it depends on the market's continued positive assessment of the borrower, the liquidity of the borrower's paper, and the borrower's compliance with market rules. If circumstances lead to price volatility in foreign markets, new placements will be inhibited.

In some East Asian countries (China, Indonesia, Korea, and Thailand), domestic banks have been major issuers of bonds into external markets. Since 1990, 40 percent of placements have been by financial institutions, with banks accounting for 27 percent. Large banks obviously have better credit ratings than many of their clients and are thus able to raise funds less expensively. This is a legitimate intermediation function and has opened financing opportunities to many domestic firms that would otherwise have had less access to funds. For the ultimate borrower, lower interest rates, not foreign exchange rates, are typically the critical factor. For the intermediating banks, the spreads and volumes are attractive, and the operations help establish the banks' international presence. These actions, however, pose two risks. First, there may be a relative decrease in the effectiveness of monetary policy, since the financial system can mitigate or offset government attempts to expand or contract credit by modulating its foreign borrowing for domestic clients. When foreign interest rates are lower than domestic rates, borrowers will be tempted to seek more funds abroad, which may undermine domestic policies of monetary restraint. Second, banks (especially public or quasi-public banks) may be borrowing abroad with the implicit or explicit expectation of a government guarantee. They may not take full account of the exchange risk and may face interest risks as well, since they are intermediating across currencies and between short-term liabilities and long-term assets. These risks are likely to be passed on to the government, should they adversely affect the banks. The recently reported instance of BAPINDO, a troubled Indonesian bank that borrowed internationally, seems to have involved an implicit guarantee, as that bank would not have been able to borrow on its own account. More generally, central banks may be forced to intervene to protect the banking sector with official reserves if there are major disruptions of commercial banks' capacity to refinance abroad. For some large borrowers, domestic markets may not yet be deep enough to absorb the size and other requirements of their financing needs, so that these enterprises must turn to international markets.

FPI in domestic markets is a different matter. The bulk of this inflow has been in equities, as investors have been seeking high yields, mostly through appreciation. These flows purchase existing portfolio assets and sometimes new issues. To the extent that the new issues fund new investment, the effects would be quite similar to those of FDI, although the physical asset would be owned by the domestic issuer rather than the foreign investor.[14] New issues may also be used to recapitalize existing operations. Here the effect would be through the banking system and the rest of the domestic financial market, where debt would be retired by the new equity-generated flows. Although this could ease pressure on the banking system, it would tend to lower interest rates and increase domestic liquidity. That, in turn, would increase aggregate demand and create more pressure on the exchange rate than if the funds had been invested in new equipment with a high import content.

The bulk of equity investment has been into existing stocks in East Asian markets, driving up the prices of equity. The cost of capital drops for those floating new issues, but there are also strong wealth effects on existing asset holders—as their wealth increases, consumption is likely to go up as well. This will tend to raise domestic prices and appreciate the currency in real terms. Whether these foreign equity investments increase physical investment depends on the behavior of the other asset holders—those who sold to foreign investors and those whose assets appreciated. If they invest in new projects, physical investment will also increase; otherwise, it will not. It is more likely that domestic savings will fall when there are large portfolio investment flows than when the flows take the form of FDI. In Latin America, which has experienced more portfolio inflows than FDI, domestic savings have tended to decline, rather than physical investment to increase. In the past East Asia has avoided this result, partly because its overall policy regime has favored investment, partly because of the greater degree of sterilization it has been able to achieve, and partly because the share of portfolio investment has been smaller.[15] Portfolio flows are a very recent phenomenon, and it is still too soon to measure many of their effects in East Asia.

It is particularly worrisome when large private capital flows move into commercial real estate. Experience in many countries, both industrial and developing, indicates the ease with which speculative bubbles can develop in real estate during an investment boom. Asset inflation in this sector can generate very high rates of return—much higher than are available from investment in manufacturing—over a few years. But such rates are not sustainable. When the bottom falls out, as it inevitably does, there are frequently severe repercussions in the banking sector, since domestic banks are usually major financiers of the real estate, and governments often end up bailing out the financial sector. Indonesia faced this problem in 1993; Thailand saw earlier bouts of these bubbles; and they are not unknown in other countries, including the United States and Japan.

The sustainability of flows into stock markets is a complex matter. To the extent that the flows depend on continued high gains, mostly appreciation, one could wonder whether the high rates of return of 1992–93 will resume after the 1994 correction. Even in the best of circumstances, one would expect some flow reversals, in addition to normal volatility. Unfortunately, the best of circumstances rarely occurs, and the Mexican episode of December 1994 has precipitated outflows in many emerging markets as fund managers have bailed out everywhere. It is hard not to view this as herd behavior with a tinge of panic, but it caused a 3 percent devaluation in Thailand and more than doubled short-term interest rates there. Other East Asian markets have also suffered outflows as international investors have generally reduced their exposure in emerging markets. However, given the long-term growth potential of the East Asian economies and the indications of a longer-term stock adjustment process, there is reason to expect that such reactions will be temporary setbacks in a persistent trend toward a larger share of sound emerging market stocks in global portfolios. The spectacular yields witnessed recently may not be sustainable, but the East Asian countries should offer high rates of return over the long term and should continue to attract investment.

A number of countries in East Asia and elsewhere have begun attracting foreign portfolio investors into their own fixed-income markets, purchasing instruments in local currency. In this case the foreign bondholder takes the exchange risk, for which he expects added compensation. It is encouraging that these economies are becoming attractive enough, and their exchange management is considered stable enough, to attract investment in local currency securities. For obvious reasons, interest tends to be in bank deposits, in shorter maturities, and in guaranteed instruments of governments or their agencies.

To the extent that short-term capital flows exceed working balances, trade financing, or bridge activities to long-term investment, they are most likely the result of relatively high interest rates not offset by an expected devaluation. For the most part, these flows are seeking high short-term rates of return and reflect cash management or speculative decisions rather than long-term investment decisions. But like long-term flows, they tend to lower domestic interest rates and appreciate the exchange rate. They are likely to expand bank reserves and lead to more credit expansion, although on a potentially more volatile base. To the extent that a government is trying to restrain domestic demand with high interest rates, the inflow would undermine its policy. These flows may not directly influence long-term savings and investment, but they may do so indirectly through their effects on interest rates and other variables. They are potentially the easiest to reverse and in the short term may have a relatively large impact on policymaking, particularly monetary policy.[16]

Other Factors

A key question is how much portfolio investment capital markets can effectively absorb and convert into real capital expansion, rather than asset inflation or simple reserve accumulation. There are no firm cutoff points. Beyond a given rate of inflow, effective utilization of the capital becomes difficult, as evidenced by rapid reserve accumulation, high rates of sterilization, or undesirably rapid real exchange rate appreciation. Under these circumstances countries may want to modulate portfolio flows to preserve stability. The potential volatility of external portfolio investment in domestic capital markets poses a double concern. First, substantial flows into and out of the country can have short-term effects on the exchange rate, interest rates, and uncertainty that then lead to longer-term negative effects on the structure of investment. In particular, expectations of fluctuating exchange rates may discourage export-oriented investment. Second, volatility in portfolio investment has a multiplier effect on domestic asset values, directly and through domestic credit levels, and this may lead to large swings in domestic demand and consumption through wealth effects.

If the government or the private sector comes to depend on FPI, continued access to foreign markets is essential. The confidence of international investors in the borrowers and, more important, in the country must be maintained. Beyond the overall macroeconomic indicators, investors must be assured that the obligor of debt or issuer of equity will be able and will be allowed to purchase the foreign exchange required to make payments—which is a national, not a firm-specific, issue.[17] When firms borrow and attract investment from abroad, governments have an interest in monitoring the extent of such liabilities because the country's total foreign obligation can affect its perceived creditworthiness. Traditional concerns about eventual repayment of obligations still apply, but the proliferation of instruments renders conventional credit indicators much less reliable for governments and independent analysts. Recent payment delays by local authorities in China have cooled investor interest in that country in general and are beginning to have negative repercussions on the government's credit standing, even though the central government tried to be clear that it was not providing a guarantee.

Where the bulk of private capital inflows is in the form of FDI or equity, there is no explicit contractual repayment obligation. Thus formal measures of external creditworthiness, such as the debt-service ratio, diminish in relevance as indicators of a country's ability to meet its external obligations. These indicators were developed when debt was the primary form of external obligation and the ability to meet contractual obligations was considered of great importance, particularly to official creditors. Equity obligations were small and were not considered essential for credit ratings.[18] Now the ability to repatriate capital is essential for maintaining access to capital markets. Since World War II there has not been a significant problem for FDI; private investors were able to repatriate dividends and capital from countries not making loan payments, even during the debt crisis. But we have relatively little recent experience with such large investment flows into developing countries. (The prewar debt crisis did involve portfolio investment, mostly bonds.) Because of high investor interest, overfinancing, and accumulation of reserves, potential problems have been at least postponed. The East Asian countries' performance record has been excellent so far. Nevertheless, it would be useful to have an indicator for a country's ability to meet expected payments on its total external obligations, comparable to the debt-service ratio or the debt-to-exports ratio traditionally used for debt.

The World Bank has undertaken some initial work in this direction, and a first-cut indicator of the sustainability of a trend toward acquiring new external obligations has been developed (Dadush, Dhareshwar, and Johannes 1994). This indicator, the asymptotic liability-to-export ratio (ALE), has been constructed in a manner analogous to the debt-to-exports ratio. Since payments on equity are contingent, it is not feasible to construct a ratio of external obligations service to exports comparable to the debt-service ratio. The ALE compares the estimated change in the country's total external liabilities with the growth rate of exports. (It would be preferable to base an indicator on the stock of total liabilities, but no estimate of that figure is readily available.) A five-year average of current account deficits is calculated as an indicator of the change in total net external obligations and is divided by the change in export earnings over the same period. Because of the lack of sufficient information on past periods of financial distress attributable to difficulties in meeting obligations on equity (separately from general capital control issues), it has not been possible to empirically determine satisfactory or worrisome levels of this ratio. But by analogy with the debt-export ratio, a value of 2 or greater would be cause for concern. Table 4.1 shows recent estimates of the ALE for a number of countries receiving large capital inflows. At this time, East Asian countries do not seem to be in danger.

It can be shown that if the rate of growth of exports (in nominal terms) is less than the average rate of return on external liabilities, any growth of external obligations is not indefinitely sustainable. This is a limiting condition; assumptions about the time path of net exports would define tighter sustainability

Rising nondebt investment is not a problem for East Asian countries.

TABLE 4.1   ASYMPTOTIC LIABILITY-TO-EXPORT RATIO AND ITS COMPONENTS, SELECTED COUNTRIES, 1989–93
(percent)

Country	Annual export growth	Ratio of current account deficit to exports	Ratio of asymptotic liability to exports
Argentina	5.7	21.4	3.7
Brazil	3.3	3.3	1.0
Chile	10.3	3.6	0.3
China	14.1	−7.1	−0.5
India	6.5	25.4	4.0
Indonesia	11.5	9.8	0.9
Korea, Rep. of	7.3	3.8	0.5
Malaysia	14.2	5.1	0.4
Mexico	8.6	28.5	3.3
Philippines	11.0	13.0	1.2
Thailand	16.5	17.7	1.1
Turkey	10.4	3.0	0.3
Venezuela	7.4	−8.8	−1.2
Median for listed countries	10.3	5.1	0.9
Median for all developing countries	7.3	15.3	1.8

Source: Dadush, Dhareshwar, and Johannes (1994).

conditions. Note that this is a generalization of the sustainability condition for debt. Continuing high export growth is clearly a necessary condition for sustaining capital inflows. What is important is to focus policymakers' attention on how to estimate the potential effects of accumulating foreign liabilities on a country's future repayment capacity and creditworthiness. The ALE is still relatively untested, and further work is needed to improve the available indicators and their interpretations for recipient countries.

So far, we have discussed the characteristics of different instruments and their impacts on various East Asian markets. Sustainability has been a major focus, and it might be interesting to see whether much can be determined on this issue from the investors' characteristics. At the outset, one must admit there may not be much that can be said; even investors' identities may not be known, and their nationality is less and less relevant. We might, however, derive some useful insights from the kinds of policies or states of the world that would increase investor's "stickiness"—that is, what is the likelihood investors will stick with a country in their investment portfolios?

Direct investors, once in place, are likely to be naturally sticky. There is a large psychological, as well as physical, investment that may be difficult to divest in the short run. However, when firms become listed in securities markets, the inherent stickiness is reduced. Profits from FDI are less sticky and can be repatriated as easily as reinvested.[19] Portfolio investors are by their nature less sticky; their involvement is more distant and their investments more liquid. Building a sustainable base of relatively more sticky investors in foreign markets requires the same kind of macroeconomic stability and successful growth policy required for FDI. In addition, portfolio investors appreciate a liquid and stable market in a country's obligations. Whether for government or private securities, sufficient depth and new issues in the market are necessary to maintain investor appetite and provide enough liquidity to permit individual investors to readily adjust their portfolios. As more institutional investors become interested in emerging markets, and as more funds are created specifically to invest in these markets, liquidity and depth will improve in aggregate and in particular markets. Country-specific funds may trade a lot of issues, but they are likely to be relatively sticky in a country. Somewhat ironically, as markets in a country's securities, both domestic and abroad, become more liquid, the country becomes more attractive for the less sticky investors—those who are concerned about the possibility of exit if their evaluations change. Experts in these markets emphasize that a flourishing domestic capital market deep in domestic investors is reassuring to foreign portfolio investors.

For obvious reasons, local investors are likely to be the stickiest of all. Indeed, when local investors place their funds abroad in substantial amounts rather than in domestic investment, this should be a warning, based on informed local knowledge, that something may be amiss. This is not to argue for restrictions on investment overseas by nationals, which can be evaded in most cases anyway. In a well-functioning market, there should be two-way flows, and, particularly in smaller markets, rational portfolio choice would argue for international diversification. But when investing abroad appears to be more capital flight than portfolio balance, serious problems in the local market may need to be addressed.[20] For a variety of domestic institutional investors, such as pension funds, regulations about permissible investments may add to stickiness, but such regulations are likely to distort the investments of these institutions if they are too strongly binding, and they should be designed carefully.[21]

Short-term deposits and bonds are probably the least sticky of the various forms of capital inflow. They are contractually the most liquid, and they can move quickly in case of alarm, real or perceived. Sound economic conditions are important, but investors in these instruments tend to be less affected by longer-term fundamentals and more responsive to short-term factors such as relative interest rates, the exchange rate, political uncertainty, or expectations about these variables. Change or expected change in these variables can trigger sharp movements in short-term capital flows, and even the threat of movements in short-term capital can restrict government action on other policy variables. It is these flows that pose the greatest dilemma for policymakers. They contribute the least to a country's long-run investment and development, but they pose the greatest challenge for managing open capital markets. Governments are most likely to want to control these flows, particularly while their own markets are still maturing. Obviously, any such actions carry the risk of introducing broader distortions and should be handled with care.

Individual portfolio investors, particularly those investing in international markets, tend to vote with their feet and exert little influence on government policies. The advent of large-scale institutional investors (mutual or pension funds) has changed that equation. These asset managers control large amounts of funds and can move substantial volumes quickly. Because of their size, compared with that of many developing country markets, and because of their sensitivity to returns in the short as well as the long term, they tend to take a more active interest in factors affecting their securities' values and may try to pressure governments into following policies favorable to their investments, either directly or through "timely" movement of funds.[22] Countries may end up facing a kind of capital market conditionality as these funds become more important to their stability.

Investment stickiness was once thought to be associated with the term of the instruments held—the stickier investors would invest in long-term instruments, and less sticky investors would buy short-term investments. This may have been true in earlier times in industrial country markets; low levels of market liquidity, high transaction costs, and low volatility would have encouraged this approach. But those conditions are less relevant today. Technological advances, market growth, and the evolution of sophisticated instruments and trading strategies, along with external events that have increased volatility, have driven most investors to trading strategies whereby all instruments and markets are continually analyzed for short-term profit opportunities. There may be instruments with long maturities, but few instruments are bought to be held long term.

While the movement to short-term trading strategies is widespread, the particular strategies employed vary from market to market, depending on the governing rules and instruments available. As markets become more evolved—with more instruments, better-defined yield curves, and more actors—the number and the variety of trading options increase. An increase in trading options enhances market liquidity and efficiency and generally promotes the market's further development. However, opportunities for speculation in the market also increase, which implies a need for adequate regulation and prudential requirements. This issue will be addressed in the next chapter.

How a market develops, including the orderly introduction of new instruments, is an important element of managing capital flows. In a broader sense, the kinds of instruments available and favored (by the tax structure or by other regulations) in a market and the extent of foreign ownership allowed may also have an effect on the allocation of investment in the real sector. For example, in markets in which bonds are readily available or pension funds are important buyers, more capital is likely to be available for long-gestating projects.

Two conclusions emerge from this analysis. First, capital flows are inherently neither good nor bad. They have a great potential to be either, depending on how productively they are used or on whether they are allowed to distort economic incentives and decisions. The contrast between growth in East Asia and stagnation in Latin America is instructive in this regard. (There are significant exceptions to this generalization in both regions—the Philippines, Chile, and Colombia come to mind.) Second, realizing positive benefits from capital inflows depends on sound macroeconomic and sectoral policies in the recipient country. Capital flows are a complement to good policy, not a substitute for it.

Notes

1."Some recent research indicates the possibility of hysteresis effects: a large short-term capital inflow and subsequent reversal may have lasting effects on an economy's growth path, which may not return to the status quo ex ante even if the capital movements are symmetrical.

2. Even so, countries may feel they are the object of some kind of "play" and resort to direct actions, as Malaysia did earlier this year.

3. See IMF (1995b) for an authoritative discussion of speculative attacks and use of short-term capital.

4. Much of the discussion of financial liberalization has used the term *deregulation* because the process involved dismantling regulations that were directly fixing interest rates, allocating credit, and so on. The use of this term has led to some confusion. Liberalized markets require indirect and prudential regulation establishing rules of behavior (capital ratios, portfolio lending limits, and disclosure, among others) to operate effectively. These regulations and the supporting supervisory institutions need to be installed in conjunction with the market liberalization.

5. The initial models fueled the debate among industrial countries in the 1960s over the relative merits of fixed or floating exchange rates as a way of pursuing independent domestic policies, leading many to conclude that floating rates allowed more independence. This was one critical factor in the general shift away from fixed rates in the early 1970s, although few countries have allowed a completely free float.

6. In a simple model, substitutability of assets is approximately equivalent to an open capital account. In the real world this may not be the case. A variety of specific

characteristics (for example, tax liabilities) or restrictions on foreign ownership of domestic assets may reduce substitutability of assets, even when capital accounts are open.

7. When foreign and domestic goods become perfect substitutes as well, fiscal policy has no effect on output. Increased integration does reduce the scope for policy independence.

8. In the long run an appreciation and a shift in the industrial and export structures are inevitable as economies maintain high rates of growth, as has happened in Japan, Korea, and Taiwan (China). The issue is the timing. Premature appreciation may slow growth and shift FDI and its growth stimulus to other economies in the region or elsewhere.

9. In fact, investors' views about country (sovereign) risk and exchange risk are a major factor in reducing the degree of substitutability between domestic and foreign assets. The larger these risks, the larger the potential for variance between domestic and international rates.

10. For example, the sharp rise in interest rates in 1981–82 was a major factor contributing to the debt crisis. It is now possible to purchase some hedges, but they tend to be expensive for developing countries and are little used.

11. There need not be a one-to-one link between the amount of FDI and the resulting increase in imports. The total size of the investment is likely to be larger than the FDI, which would be supplemented by local funding. The import component of the investment project, however, could be less than one. Thus the ultimate ratio of FDI to resulting capital imports will vary from project to project. Whether it is large or small is of some interest to policymakers in the aggregate.

12. Assuming that a country is able to attract 2 percent of its GDP annually in FDI over twenty years, that the incremental capital-output ratio (ICOR) is four, and that the economy is growing at 8 percent per year—a typical East Asian performance—foreign investors would end up owning less than 5 percent of the economy's total capital stock at the end of the period. However, since it is unlikely that ownership would be spread evenly throughout the economy, the concentration of foreign ownership may be much greater in some (probably export) sectors.

13. In balance of payments statistics, all earned profits on FDI are reported as outflow. If the profits are reinvested, they are counted as inflow, although they may never have physically left the country. Therefore, estimating new flows—as contrasted with reinvestment of profits—is often difficult. New flows are likely to fluctuate more than reinvestments.

14. Weak listing and disclosure rules may not prevent fraud in some instances, in which case the funds could be directed anywhere. However, this is not the fault of the foreign investment but of the regulatory system.

15. Longer histories of price stability and low deficits have made it easier for governments to issue bonds at reasonable interest rates in East Asia than in Latin America.

16. Some recent research has indicated that it is not possible to distinguish between various maturity instruments in terms of their volatility. However, short-term instruments have to be refinanced more frequently and expose the issuer to market fluctuations more often (see Claessens, Dooley, and Warner 1995).

17. Credit ratings take the issue of confidence into account. Rarely is an enterprise in a country given a rating higher than the country's rating, and then only if it has independent access to foreign exchange earnings. One factor contributing to the debt crisis in the 1980s was the lenders' realization that borrowing countries in total had a higher level of debt than was believed when the individual loans were made.

18. Mineral extraction investments were a partial exception to this generalization and were often important for a small number of countries. However, dividends and profits were usually repatriated through exports of the mineral itself, and the issue more frequently raised was whether the country was getting a fair deal.

19. A variety of techniques allow firms to transfer funds covertly. And imaginative financing can permit direct investors to withdraw their capital surprisingly fast.

20. This tell-tale sign was missed or ignored in the Latin American debt crisis of the past decade. Substantial amounts of bank lending simply fueled domestic capital flight, contributing to the later crisis. It also appears that the recent Mexican crisis was precipitated by nationals moving into dollars, exploiting local knowledge or intuition.

21. In countries with limited capital markets, requiring provident funds to invest only locally can distort local markets and lead to illiquid markets. If the provident fund were to own most of the market's securities, who would trade with whom? In some cases, these funds are directed to invest in government bonds, but this raises issues of adequate budget management and use of the provident fund to finance a government deficit, which in itself is not sustainable.

22. The *Wall Street Journal* reported on June 14, 1994 (p. 1, in an article by Craig Torres and Thomas T. Vogel), that managers of major U.S.-based funds had made strong representations to the Mexican government concerning macroeconomic policy actions they considered essential if they were to maintain their investment levels in Mexico. These actions included, in effect, an exchange rate guarantee.

CHAPTER FIVE

Regulatory and Infrastructure Issues

Establishing an appropriate regulatory structure and infrastructure for financial markets and transactions is absolutely essential to managing the large capital inflows East Asian countries are experiencing, particularly the portfolio flows. It is equally important to ensure that the regulatory, tax, and legal structures provide appropriate incentives for prudent behavior by agents in the financial sector. These are necessary concomitants to the liberalization taking place. Markets need a core set of regulations and infrastructure to maintain orderly behavior in order to attract long-term investors and protect all participants from various types of fraud. A review of all financial infrastructure and regulations for East Asian capital markets is beyond the scope of this chapter, which focuses on the underlying rationale for regulation and on selected issues that will enable a country to integrate more effectively with international capital markets. Particular attention is paid to measures that enhance the sustainability of foreign capital flows, reduce the potential for market disruptions, and eliminate impediments to efficiency in a global environment. In general, policymakers need to confine their interventions to those that are necessary for alleviating market failures and to avoid interventions that can become market supplanting and thus distorting.

Rationales for Regulation

Casual observation tells us that despite extensive government interventions in financial markets, financial crises have shaken many economies, including

Chile, Hong Kong, Malaysia, Mexico, and the United States. Fundamentally, financial markets are different from goods markets. In the latter a good or service is exchanged for another (or for money, which is a claim on current goods) at the same time. In financial markets the basic transaction is an immediate exchange of a good (or equivalently, money) against a promise (by way of some contractual instrument) to return goods or money at some time in the future and perhaps contingent on certain future events. Uncertainty and risk are inevitably part of the transaction. For any transaction across time, risk is related to the likelihood that the future end of the transaction will be completed. International transactions are also affected by uncertainties regarding differences in rules and procedures governing transactions in different jurisdictions and possible exchange rate changes. These uncertainties flow in part from lack of information. Although information is essential to rational decisionmaking, it is often costly to obtain; it may be asymmetrically available (for example, between borrower and lender); and it is always incomplete—necessarily so about the future. Financial markets are particularly sensitive to information; partial or differential access to it can result in significant market imperfections and inefficiency. Another critical factor for well-functioning capital markets, including direct investment, is definition of ownership rights, transaction rules, and enforcement procedures. These can only be ensured by the government.

The rationales for government intervention in markets, even after liberalization, have stemmed largely from the above considerations, together with a general concern that governments have a responsibility for preventing or mitigating systemic crises. Financial sectors are critical to a well-functioning economy, and their public good element justifies public involvement. Unfortunately, government intervention can also distort the behavior of market participants in undesirable ways, so a delicate balance must be achieved between interventions that alleviate market failures and the potential negative impacts of these interventions.

Information

Markets can function efficiently only when information is readily and generally available to participants. When information is costly, markets in general are not fully competitive and the market equilibrium is not optimal. In the financial sector costly information can give rise to other market failures, in the form of externalities and absent or incomplete markets—a common situation in developing countries as well as in economies in transition. (This section draws on Stiglitz 1994 and Levine 1994.)

Information can be so costly (or transaction costs so high) as to limit trade or prevent the existence of some markets (see, for example, the model of "lemons" in Akerlof 1970). Information costs tend to be higher for foreign investors acting through international financial markets. These investors are likely to know much less about default risk, interest risk, country risk, and perhaps exchange rate risk than local agents or borrowers, which helps account for their slow penetration into emerging markets until recently. Furthermore, in financial markets borrowers and lenders have asymmetric access to information: the borrower knows much more about the nature and risks involved in his firm or an investment project than the lender, but the lender may know more about the true costs of funds in external markets. Examples of information deficiencies leading to missing or incomplete markets are the following:

■ *Equity issuance.* The information asymmetry between firm insiders and outsiders can discourage the raising of capital through equity issuance. Outsiders may perceive that insiders would be willing to sell shares only if the price were higher than the "real" value. Or insiders are thought to possess other information or options that will allow them to profit at the expense of the outsider, especially where accounting practices are not formalized and enforced. Even in some industrial countries, equity markets are weak where information is not readily available (Greenwald, Stiglitz, and Weiss 1984).

■ *The missing long-term bond market.* Bond markets depend both on information and on adequate contract enforcement procedures, which may be lacking in emerging markets. Furthermore, long-term bonds require that the investors be confident that issuers will remain solvent over a long enough period. In emerging markets few firms yet have much of a track record. These factors may have contributed to the lack of a complete yield curve in East Asia, where market rates for long-term interest are often undetermined, encouraging would-be borrowers to issue bonds abroad where possible.

Monitoring

Among the major functions of financial intermediaries are to select among alternative projects and to monitor firms' use of funds. Monitoring of financial intermediaries themselves is also crucial for the financial system's soundness and the health of the whole economy. However, information is costly, and monitoring has a large public good element. Thus it is likely that the private sector would not sufficiently monitor firms or financial intermediaries in the absence of government intervention. Indeed, banks may not seek adequate information if they are lending at government direction or to "friendly" firms, especially if they are not ultimately held responsible for losses. (The "too-important-to-fail" syndrome occurs in emerging markets as well.) A number of financial sectors in East Asia have been weakened by a variety of policies that constrain interest rates, direct a substantial portion of lending, or discourage adequate supervision of lending (all varieties of financial repression). Most countries in the region are now introducing reforms to strengthen their banking systems and reduce financial repression.

Insufficient monitoring has serious social consequences. It can exacerbate the principal-agent problem of the firms and intermediaries, so that managers do not act in the best interest of shareholders or creditors.[1] In turn this problem may threaten the financial system's soundness and lead to insolvency of financial institutions. Inadequate monitoring adds to investor risk and is likely to discourage foreign investors, who are least able to undertake sufficient monitoring on their own. Failures of financial intermediaries have large negative economic and social impacts that reach beyond the creditors of the failed institution, often imposing high costs on the government in the ensuing rescue operation. Systemic failures with serious real sector consequences are the nightmare of many experts and policymakers.

Imperfect Competition

In the financial sector, competition is often limited because of differences in the information available to buyers and sellers and high costs of or explicit limits on entry. Reduced competition diminishes efficiency and may lead to other welfare losses. For example:

■ When information is imperfect, lenders cannot make rational credit decisions or monitor borrowers' behavior. Raising interest rates to try to clear the market may cause an adverse selection of firms in the loan market.[2] Good firms drop out; firms with big default risks stay. Firms may then engage in highly risky activities, creating moral hazard.[3] The borrower that is willing to pay the highest interest rate may not be the one with the highest risk-adjusted expected rate of return to the lenders because of a higher probability of default. Thus, to maximize their expected profits, lenders often charge an interest rate lower than the market-clearing level while rationing credit to those they can evaluate. Overall credit constraints with interest controls have similar effects. When a project or an enterprise is unknown, it may get rationed out of the credit market, whereas a customer with a long track record or with good collateral but a less promising project may get financed because the lender's private return can be easily assessed and assured. Failure of apparently promising projects to obtain financing is often used as a rationale for directed financing; however, without good project evaluation, directed credit may aggravate the moral hazard and weaken the balance sheets of financial intermediaries.

■ Banks and creditors rely more heavily on long-term customer relations than they would if better information were available. Since borrowers know more about the nature of their business and the risks involved than lenders, banks and other lenders often specialize in certain sectors or regions. They rely heavily on long-term customer relations to minimize their risks and cost of information. This is an underlying factor in the development of the "main bank" system in Japan and the "small home-town bank" approach in the United States. Here again, the credit market may not be able to allocate the loanable funds where the social return is the highest. In dealing with international markets, these factors become all the more important.

Although the above examples refer to largely domestic financial market issues, these problems are important to foreign investors. Domestic imperfections shape the range and quality of investment choices available to the foreign investor and the confidence accorded available market information. For FDI investors, some of these factors are less critical because the investor is a party to creating the project itself. However, if the FDI investor is relying on domestic finance to help support his project, the efficacy of the domestic financial sector is important in attracting and maintaining FDI. Portfolio investment on a large scale is a much more recent phenomenon and depends even more on a well-functioning domestic capital market, one where the imperfections noted above are not excessive. The recent flows are testing East Asia's financial markets and accelerating reforms. How fast and securely the reforms can be implemented will have a large effect on how well portfolio flows can be sustained. The countries in East Asia that have been best able to manage large capital inflows, such as Malaysia and Thailand, have also gone the furthest in reforming and liberalizing their financial sectors.

Government Roles

Even in liberalized markets, governments have a central role in mitigating the above problems. In particular, the government can:

■ Compel the disclosure of information or collect and disseminate information and thus reduce information costs and alleviate asymmetries

■ Establish minimum financial viability requirements and enforcement mechanisms to lay the basis for trust and security in financial dealings

■ Monitor the behavior of market participants—firms or financial intermediaries—through the design, enactment, and enforcement of legislation and regulations

- Set up basic institutions—such as development banks for long-term loans, credit rating agencies, and insurance companies—at the early stage of development, when these are missing, and thus replicate the services of absent market segments[4]

- Take responsibility for maintaining macroeconomic stability to lessen the risk of insolvencies and thereby reduce the externalities of failures.

Governments can exercise their authority in these areas through the various instrumentalities of the ministry of finance, the central bank, or other public bodies responsible for capital market activities. Experience has shown that greater independence accorded to central banks, when these responsibilities are clearly defined, tends to foster more stable policies and less financial repression.

Government interventions, however, have their limitations. Governments may encourage the production of information, but they are not necessarily more efficient than the private sector in using that information to assess risks and evaluate projects. When markets are not yet well developed, governments may also provide missing insurance or other services, but they must be sure to avoid implicit or explicit subsidies, especially where market agents rather than the government determine the extent and amounts of protection without fully bearing the costs.[5] Decisionmakers need to limit their interventions to those that are necessary for mitigating market failures. Interventions should not become a market-supplanting mechanism or distort market-determined prices and allocations. Rather, they should be designed to support the orderly development of markets and to correct market failures.

Basic Market Infrastructure and Regulation

Key areas for facilitating effective absorption, allocation, and management of foreign inflows include the establishment of (a) a legal structure that defines rules on ownership, auditing, and disclosure; (b) prudential regulations and appropriate enforcement procedures; (c) an effective operating infrastructure for completing transactions, transferring ownership, and settling balances; (d) appropriate incentives for financial agents and institutions; and (e) adequate collection and dissemination of financial data. Strengthening and expanding the underlying infrastructure facilitates the development of effective capital markets, which will make them more attractive to foreign investors, increase their ability to absorb capital flows, and give governments better tools for managing capital flows without (or with less) recourse to distorting direct interventions or expensive subsidies or guarantees (in whatever form). The process of building market infrastructure, establishing the necessary regulatory and monitoring institutions, and training competent staff is a long one that requires constant support from the authorities.

Legal Structure

All countries in East Asia have imposed constraints on foreign ownership of assets (land, enterprises, equity, and other financial assets) as part of their financial sector and other development policies. These controls have ranged from outright prohibition to requirements for joint ownership and eventual divestiture. Even where capital accounts have been open, capital inflows have been constrained and their allocation affected by these ownership restrictions. As East Asian economies have become more mature and have developed substantial national wealth and entrepreneurs, they have progressively liberalized their ownership rules. That liberalization has been a major factor in the rapid expansion of FDI and portfolio investment in the region. Privatization programs depend in many instances on further opening of ownership rules. For economies in transition in the region, the process of defining and expanding the scope for private ownership of assets and firms is in its early stages. The influx of large amounts of foreign investment in China is accelerating the pace of this process there. In Viet Nam legal system reforms were initiated very early in the transition process.

Restrictions on foreign ownership have been slowest to ease in the financial sector itself. Arguments for maintaining them range from protection of infant industry to "national interests." The restrictions represent major obstacles to attracting foreign capital and integrating into the global capital market. Openness to foreign banks and nonbank financial institutions is an important condition for attracting FDI and portfolio investment. Foreign investors usually feel more comfortable dealing with familiar financial institutions with which they can also do business elsewhere. Moreover, the presence of foreign firms in a domestic market contributes to its efficiency and to its adaptation of international standards to fit local circumstances. International money center banks often provide a wide range of services for interfacing with world markets that are not available from domestic banks. These services are critically important to the development of local capital and money markets, as well as to international investors. The technology is usually spread rapidly from foreign to domestic financial institutions, and foreign-owned institutions provide valuable training for nationals.

More and more governments have started permitting greater foreign competition in their financial sectors. It is not a coincidence that Singapore, which is among the most advanced financial centers in East Asia, also has the highest foreign penetration in its banking system. In 1992 foreign banks accounted for 73 percent of Singapore's total trade-financing business and 64 percent of total banking profit. In the domestic market foreign banks account for almost half of all deposits from residents and more than half of all loans to residents (US ASEAN Council 1994, p. 16). Furthermore, membership on the Stock Exchange of Singapore was recently opened to foreign firms, although foreign ownership is still limited to a fixed percentage in Singapore banks and to certain companies deemed to be of strategic importance. Foreign banks also have a large presence in Malaysia, accounting for sixteen of thirty-eight licensed banks, a quarter of total bank loans, and a fifth of total bank deposits. China's first national law for foreign financial institutions, the Regulations on Financial Institutions with Foreign Investment, which came into effect April 1, 1994, stipulates five types of operations that may be set up by foreign financial institutions. The types include foreign-owned banks or finance companies with head offices in China, Sino-foreign joint venture banks and financial companies, and branches of foreign banks.

Liberalization of rules governing ownership must be founded on a secure and transparent legal structure and broad market infrastructure that include basic accounting rules, auditing institutions, and a body of corporate and securities law. These features assure stock and bond holders, who do not have direct control of the corporation, of access to information with which to evaluate a firm's performance. One impediment to participation by developing countries in the international capital market is that their accounting rules often do not conform to international standards. Accounting and auditing agencies are major information producers in capital markets. By measuring and reporting the operational condition of corporations issuing securities, they provide crucial information to investors on the quality of the securities, expected earning potentials, and risks. If accounting and auditing rules are incomplete or inconsistent across countries, investors cannot ascertain the true meaning of the reports provided or can do so only at great cost, which makes evaluation of investments much more difficult. These failings exacerbate information asymmetry, reduce investor confidence, and sap the attractiveness of domestic issues to international investors.

For example, China's accounting and statistical system used to be completely different from that in market economies. It was confusing to foreign investors, hindered FDI and portfolio investment, and constituted a major obstacle to setting up joint ventures and getting Chinese corporations listed on overseas exchanges. In July 1993 the enterprise accounting system was transformed in line with international standards. An auditing law went into effect in September 1994, and although China still has a long way to go in fully implementing these laws and strengthening auditing institutions, this was an important step.[6] Given the large portfolio flows moving into China, continued progress in this area is vital. Other countries in the region have also been upgrading their accounting regulations.

Any basic law on securities and exchanges must have clauses on information disclosure by the listing corporations. These clauses must specify the type, frequency, and amount of relevant information that must be honestly and publicly reported concerning operational condition, assets and liabilities, profits and losses, main business activities and investments, major shareholders, and shareholdings of the corporation's managers.

In addition to requiring market participants to supply the financial information necessary for investors to make informed judgments, well-functioning markets themselves provide vital information to assist in the efficient allocation of capital. Active stock markets offer a barometer of the returns to investment and the relative costs of raising capital. Bond markets help long-term investors raise stable funds and also provide information on prevailing equilibrium interest rates. Nothing else in a market economy is able to replace the bond market in providing this crucial information for allocating capital. The prices of long-term and short-term funds form the basis for decisions about the intertemporal transfer of resources. Market-driven yields on government bonds often serve as a risk-free benchmark rate for the financial system and enable more accurate pricing of existing instruments. In developing countries, however, bond markets are often underdeveloped, in that they do not have long-term instruments and thus lack a complete yield curve. Government bond markets are often neither open to regular trading nor free from directed placement. Thus, even where they exist, they may not provide valid interest rate information.

East Asian governments often run no budget deficits and therefore generate little debt, so there is often not sufficient trading in limited treasury bonds to set a benchmark rate. Without a market for risk-free assets, it is difficult to establish a reference rate, but other instruments can fulfill this reference function. In Thailand high-quality bonds of public utilities serve this purpose, as may central bank paper. For a full discussion of the important issue of bond market development, see World Bank (1995).

Prudential Regulation and Enforcement

Prudential regulation and supervision are crucial to maintaining the soundness of capital markets. Integrating East Asian capital markets into the global market increases the demand for financial regulation. As markets become more liberalized, the rules of the game have to be modified away from direct controls and toward indirect measures that facilitate well-functioning markets while striking a delicate balance between stability and the flexibility markets require. Several criteria are available for evaluating financial regulations: among the most important are stability, efficiency, fairness, and openness. Well-designed and well-implemented prudential regulations and supervision increase investor confidence and reduce risks. The primary regulations should cover the following elements for all financial institutions:

- Requirements for minimum capital, reserves, and bad loan reserves

- Licensing provisions on ownership and branching

- Public disclosure of information

- Operating guidelines on mergers and consolidation

- Early warning system, supervision, and examination

- Enforcement of sanctions on both firms and individuals when rules have been violated.

Additional prudential regulations would be appropriate for enterprises that issue securities and for nonbanking institutions that deal in securities, including securities dealers and brokerage firms, investment banks, finance companies, mutual funds, and other institutional investors.[7] The most important of these additional regulations would include:

- Registration and capital requirements for securities issuers

- Registration requirements for corporations to be listed on exchanges

- Restrictions on insider-trading-based information

- Rules for soliciting business by securities dealers, brokers, and mutual funds

- Regulations on, for example, margin requirements and trading of futures and options.

Stability is of prime importance for international capital flows, since an unstable financial system not only has an adverse impact on economic activities but could also cause large capital outflows. Financial stability can be enhanced by increasing capital and reserve requirements, strengthening financial supervision, and enforcing sanctions. Adequate supervision and examination in the field and an effective early-warning system are more important than simply setting up requirements on paper.

Most East Asian countries have established the basic laws needed for capital markets, but enforcement has been inconsistent. Poor law enforcement has serious consequences: it encourages mischievous behavior while appearing to oppose it. Investors' confidence falls when they do not believe their interests will be protected, and their willingness to invest in that particular market diminishes. International investors are most wary of fraud-prone markets. Their information disadvantage is aggravated, and their risks and vulnerability to market manipulation are increased. One may, however, differentiate the various rules and their enforcement according to their significance. Some basic rules, such as disclosure of information by listing corporations and prevention of outright fraud, would have to be strictly enforced. Brokers and other dealers should be subject to similar rules to maintain confidence. Other rules, such as regulations on insider trading, lie in a gray area where more variation in market practice may be tolerated if returns remain high. But even here, attracting a wider range of investors will be easier with tighter rules that promote fairness.

Effective enforcement of regulations is beginning to take hold in some East Asian emerging markets. Thailand's Securities and Exchange Commission has emphasized relatively high disclosure standards and has prosecuted market manipulators vigorously since its establishment in 1992. The crackdown has apparently sent a clear signal to the market that investors' interests will be protected, and money continues to flow into the Thai market. China's progress in this area is remarkable: in February 1994 the Shanghai branch of Xiangfan Credit & Investment, a securities broker owned by the state-run Agricultural Bank of China, was fined 2 million yuan ($230,000) and had 16 million yuan of profits confiscated for buying shares in another company on the basis of inside knowledge of a pending bid (*Economist*, July 16, 1994).

Speedy sanctions to prevent insolvent institutions from adversely affecting others are also crucial, as was shown by Malaysia's banking crisis in the mid-1980s. The Malaysian economy suffered from deflation in 1985 and 1986, and its financial system took big losses from steep falls in the prices of commodities, securities, and real estate. The authorities took decisive action to contain the losses, recapitalize banks, and restructure institutions that were unable to raise new capital. The central bank replaced the management of four commercial banks, assumed control of four finance companies, and arranged to inject capital. As a second step, the authorities introduced major changes in banking laws to emphasize prudential regulations, such as minimum capital requirements, dispersion of ownership, limits on risk concentrations, guidelines on provisions for loan losses, and improved statistical reporting to the central bank.

Nevertheless, emerging capital markets are not fully developed, and governments are often called on to fill gaps or make up for market failures. The main challenge is to devise measures that are effective without undermining competition, innovation, or the financial system's fiduciary responsibility. For example, in developing countries it is often necessary for governments to provide insurance or explicit guarantees for the safety of small savers' funds in order to attract deposits. However, if deposit insurance is used to prevent bank runs on distressed or fragile institutions, it is likely to distort incentives. Poorly designed government insurance could place a heavy fiscal burden on the government because of adverse selection and moral hazard problems. In particular, the combination of deposit insurance in any form with exchange rate guarantees is dangerous and can lead to destabilizing capital flows. By establishing well-functioning financial markets with adequate prudential regulations, governments provide adequate assurances to both savers and investors, who should be prepared to accept normal risks. As markets improve, governments should withdraw from any insurance or guarantee programs.[8] Obviously, building an effective regulatory structure and conditioning the desired behavior within the system are evolutionary processes best started as early as possible.

Operating Infrastructure

Beyond the broad issues of legal structure and market regulation lies the nitty-gritty of carrying out market transactions. Without a basic infrastructure to complete transactions reliably, capital flows very slowly. This is particularly true for portfolio investment, but onerous registration and approval procedures also discourage FDI.

One impediment to integrating emerging markets into the global capital market is slow settlement and delivery. In countries where scriptless trading has not been introduced or a computer network is not well developed, it sometimes takes three to seven days or longer for the trade to be settled and the securities to be delivered. This increases the transaction costs and risks, since market conditions could change significantly in that period. Foreign investors are concerned about the ease with which they can cash in their profits, and such delays add to their uncertainty. Singapore introduced scriptless trading in 1987, and as a result, turnover in the secondary bond market increased dramatically, from nearly nothing to the equivalent of 70 percent of GDP in 1991–92 (US ASEAN Council 1994, p. 32). Computerization and scriptless transactions in China and in Taiwan (China) have also led to high turnover, some of it undoubtedly for speculative purposes (see table 5.1). Although China's market capitalization is small (3.5 percent of GDP in 1992 and 8 percent in 1993; see table 5.2), the daily trading volume in the

Shanghai Exchange reportedly exceeded that of Hong Kong in August 1994 (IFC data).

Credit-rating agencies are an important part of market infrastructure, as well as a major source of market information. They complement the international rating agencies that evaluate sovereign risk and major borrowers. National credit-rating agencies help monitor domestic securities by classifying corporate and other bonds according to standardized ratings and implicitly evaluating corporations' prospects. They provide an objective judgment on the quality of bonds, reduce information asymmetries, monitor issues, and help maintain investor confidence. At the same time, they contribute to the convergence of market prices and facilitate evaluation of assets. Credit-rating agencies are also important for attracting foreign investment, since foreign investors are often unfamiliar with the accounting rules and corporate laws of the issuing countries. The existence of rating agencies lessens the need for investors to do independent credit analysis, and hence reduces their transaction costs.

Malaysia's government has placed strong emphasis on deepening the secondary market for private debt instruments and corporate bonds, which is facilitated by the rapidly growing ability of the credit-rating agency, Rating Agency Malaysia (RAM).[9] All debt securities issued in Malaysia must be rated by the agency. Issuance of corporate paper and bonds has surged since RAM was created. RAM rated twenty-one issues worth 2.92 billion ringgit in 1992 and seventy issues totaling 8.44 billion ringgit in 1993. By mid-May 1994 it had rated another thirty-two issues.

In July 1993 the government of Thailand established a rating agency, TRIS, to encourage the development of its corporate bond market. It has also set a ceiling for overseas borrowing by state-owned enterprises ($2.5 billion a year for all SOEs) to help manage the exposure of Thai issues in international markets. The government urges state firms to get a full rating from the new national rating agency and to issue debt without government guarantees.

Small-Market Capitalization

When an asset market is "thin," liquidity is low and transaction costs are high, both of which reduce the market's attractiveness to foreign capital. Liquidity is an important desirable feature for foreign investors, since it reduces the risks and costs associated with their eventual withdrawal from a market. Transaction costs in a thin market are high—bid-ask spreads are large—because dealers have to bear higher risks than in a deeper market. In addition, a thin market is more vulnerable to price manipulation and high volatility,

Turnover rates are high in East Asia.

TABLE 5.1 TURNOVER RATIOS IN LOCAL EQUITY MARKETS, 1985–95
(percent)

Economy	1985	1989	1990	1991	1992	1993	1994[a]	April–June, 1995
China	—	—	—	—	159.8	164.0	42.8	32.4
Indonesia	2.9	38.6	75.8	40.1	41.2	40.5	6.8	6.6
Korea, Rep. of	61.8	101.5	61.3	82.3	114.8	172.2	49.6	17.9
Malaysia	13.4	21.8	24.6	20.2	27.3	94.3	11.6	9.2
Philippines	14.1	29.1	13.5	18.8	24.8	25.1	7.8	6.5
Taiwan (China)	48.4	531.7	429.8	330.1	209.3	235.5	72.0	45.3
Thailand	32.1	78.5	92.6	102.2	153.6	91.5	10.5	13.7
Memoranda								
India	48.3	68.8	65.9	56.8	37.0	27.5	5.2	1.9
Mexico	65.8	33.3	44.0	47.9	37.0	36.8	8.7	7.9

— Not available.
Note: The turnover ratio is the total value of shares traded as a percentage of average market capitalization during the period.
a. Data are for the fourth quarter.
Source: IFC (1994, 1995).

East Asian markets are becoming more active as their capitalization rises.

TABLE 5.2 LIQUIDITY INDICATORS IN LOCAL EQUITY MARKETS, SELECTED YEARS

Economy	Market capitalization (percentage of GDP)				Value traded (percentage of market capitalization)			
	1986	1989	1993	1994	1986	1989	1993	1994[a]
China	—	—	7.8	8.6	—	—	106.9	48.4
Indonesia	—	—	23.1	30.2	—	—	27.8	6.5
Korea	10.1	55.6	42.1	50.9	99.6	103.2	160.0	48.9
Malaysia	50.9	81.3	340.0	282.7	9.3	22.6	69.7	12.5
Philippines	4.3	20.2	89.0	86.9	30.1	27.9	16.8	7.8
Taiwan (China)	19.2	160.5	—	—	137.6	465.9	177.5	68.6
Thailand	5.1	21.9	132.9	93.1	53.4	88.4	66.6	11.0
Memoranda								
India	6.1	9.5	39.0	43.8	71.0	69.3	22.3	5.3
Mexico	5.2	10.1	58.4	34.7	80.1	33.0	31.1	9.0

— Not available.
a. Data are for the fourth quarter.
Source: Bekaert (1993); IFC (1994, 1995).

since one or a few big stockholders can control with relative ease the volume of certain stocks supplied to the market. Even markets with relatively large capitalization can behave as though they were thin if most of the value is in a few large issues.

Government interventions can help increase market capitalization by, for example, privatizing SOEs, encouraging healthy corporations to seek listing on the stock market, allowing broader foreign ownership, and generally easing regulations and taxes on transactions, subject to prudential concerns. The Korean government restricted the debt-equity ratio of large firms, which substantially increased the magnitude of equity issues for domestic investors. This created a large domestic stock market, which has recently been opened to foreign investment. The pace of privatization significantly affects the depth of equity markets and foreign capital flows. In the Philippines about eighty-one government-owned and -controlled corporations had been sold by February 1994, generating 28 billion pesos in revenues and greatly increasing participation in the Manila stock market. Equity sold includes 40 percent of Petron (the state oil company), 67 percent of Philippines Airlines, and 43 percent of the Philippines National Bank. Malaysia has also undertaken an extensive privatization program covering more than 100 firms. A major objective was to diversify domestic ownership of assets rather than attract foreign investment. The experience in Latin America and in East Europe's transition economies also suggests the importance of privatization in deepening the equity market and attracting foreign investment.

When equity markets are thin, the pace and timing of new listings on the market can have a significant impact on prices. Government policies on listing can also influence markets substantially. On July 29, 1994, the China Securities Regulatory Commission announced a ban on new listings of A shares for the rest of the year and hinted that foreigners would be allowed to invest. Shares rose over 100 percent in the following days. This action was believed to be in response to concern over depressed prices, but it does raise the question of how much governments should interfere in manipulating prices.

Incentive Structure

Financial markets, international and domestic, are populated by individuals and firms seeking to maximize their own incomes and profits. Their actions and strategies are derived from the overall regulatory structure under which they operate and from the incentives structure that determines their own incomes. Thus a well-designed incentive system is important for a market's stability and smooth functioning. To a certain extent the overall regulatory structure establishes the basic do's and don't's. Moreover, basic regulations (such as what banks are allowed to do and entry requirements for banking) are important determinants of long-run profits. The details of tax policy, remuneration practice, and enforcement also have a large effect on how markets develop. Differential taxes (on, for example, capital gains versus income), different taxes on different kinds of transactions—for example, stamp taxes on sales of securities—and possibilities for avoiding taxes on certain kinds of transactions will influence the kind and frequency of transactions that take place in financial markets. Where dividends are taxed more heavily than interest, debt-equity ratios will tend to be higher; where costs on financial asset transactions are high, markets will be less active; and where off-market transactions can be structured to avoid taxes that apply to market transactions, formal markets will not be very busy. In some instances the effects of these tax structures can be substantial.

Incentive structures can also affect market efficiency and encourage prudent behavior. If most transaction fees are fixed by law or convention, there is little incentive to improve service or compete; indeed, there may be incentives to undertake unnecessary transactions to gain fees. If fees are based on transaction size rather than result, care must be taken that the parties understand where the various interests lie. For example, when the main promoters of a project-financing deal make their money as a percentage of the amount of the project and have no capital at risk, they may have an incentive to construct not the best project, but one that maximizes the basis for their fee. Incentives need to be designed to reward behavior that promotes market efficiency and to penalize behavior that does not, through, for example, fines and other sanctions for misbehavior. If individual agents are not held responsible for their actions, it is hard to make markets function effectively.

If owners of financial institutions are improperly motivated, they are likely to perform perversely. Banks are especially susceptible to this tendency, since they often function with an implicit or explicit guarantee of their liabilities. Unless bank managers and owners are rewarded for taking only prudent risks, they will invest too little effort in monitoring their own institution or will explicitly go for broke by taking excessive risks. Barings Bank stands out as an example of the former: managers and owners in London saw large profits coming in and were not motivated to investigate the risks. Similarly, Banco Latino of Venezuela and Credit Lyonnais in France are excellent examples of the latter, with Banco Latino achieving the dubious distinction of incurring losses greater than its total *assets*. High capital ratios, higher limits on the liability of bank owners, or limited entry (and therefore significant rents for bank owners, to protect banking) are alternatives for motivating bank owners to engage in behavior more consonant with sound banking. Although these considerations are most crucial in banking, they also matter in nonbank financial intermediaries, especially those whose large size leads to some expectation of government support.

Data Collection

As capital markets are liberalized and as governments increase their prudential regulations and monitoring functions in lieu of direct interventions, information requirements increase radically. Monitoring agencies should collect a large part of the information directly from the institutions they supervise (see boxes 5.1 and 5.2).[10] In addition, more information is needed from the markets themselves in order to measure flows, interest rates, and so on. Traditionally, data collection has been geared toward preparing balance of payment estimates or has been a byproduct of registration and control procedures. The former estimates strive for accuracy rather than timeliness and are often produced after a substantial lag. Registration data on private capital flows are scarce and often of poor quality. Moreover, liberalization programs have reduced the availability of data from registration and other administrative processes. The traditional systems cannot meet the need for monitoring international capital flows or domestic market activities in terms of either timeliness or scope of information. In order to monitor and ultimately manage capital flows, data collection must be upgraded. Information needs to be collected weekly or even daily on both long-term and short-term flows in the form of bank deposits, certificates of deposit (CDs) and other money market instruments, government securities, and daily volumes in bond and equity markets.

The first priorities are (a) to identify and evaluate the information available on capital flows; (b) to identify those series that could be compiled in a timely fashion; and (c) to select those that would be useful for policy analysis. Special attention should be paid to improving data collection on private short-term and medium-term capital flows, since these are poorly documented,

---

BOX 5.1   CAPITAL FLOWS TO BE MONITORED

■ Nonresident bank deposits
■ Portfolio investment (on exchanges and private placements): institutional and individual (direct private investment)
■ Purchases of local-currency money market securities

■ Purchases of land and buildings
■ Funds from domestic companies listing abroad
■ Funds from official aid from abroad
■ Commercial borrowing abroad by domestic entities (both state and private)

---

quickly disbursed, and, in many cases, linked to corresponding outflows, such as dividends, profits, royalties, and rents. Many types of private flows react quickly to current factors, such as short-term interest rate differentials, new public offerings, and the investment policies of foreign mutual funds. For some data series, daily monitoring may be essential.

To improve data collection, close cooperation among key public financial institutions, regulatory agencies, and various securities markets is essential. When information sharing is difficult because of interagency rivalry and power struggles, an alternative is to establish a new monetary policy body with an effective and well-trained expert staff. An early-warning system could be developed to expedite analysis and use of available data by, among other tasks, tracking key data and calculating ratios for quickly identifying trends in movements of certain categories of funds in or out of a country. Automatic reporting of certain accounts could be built into bank, nonbank, and stock exchange reporting. Eventually some statistical and econometric testing of various data series might shed light on critical factors that influence foreign capital flows. Central banks in the region are strengthening their cooperation among themselves and developing mechanisms for sharing pertinent data with each other. Countries may find that different data series are more likely to reflect significant shifts in short-term capital movements. Some investigation and experimentation might lead to a reduced set of data series that will be most readily available and useful to monetary authorities and to the market at large.

Notes

1. The principal-agent problem is a type of risk in equity contracts. When managers own only a small fraction of the firm and a majority of the equity is owned by shareholders, ownership and control are separated. This separation leads to moral hazard in which the managers in control (agent) may act in their own interest rather than in the interest of the shareholders (principal).

2. Adverse selection is a problem created by asymmetric information before the transaction occurs. Adverse selection in financial markets occurs when the potential borrowers who are most likely to produce an undesirable (adverse) outcome are the ones who most actively seek out a loan, are willing to pay higher rates, and are thus most likely to be selected.

3. Moral hazard is a problem caused by asymmetric information *after* the transaction occurs. Moral hazard occurs when the lender is subject to the possibility of a borrower having incentives to engage in activities that are undesirable from the lender's point of view.

4. Care is needed here. Government intervention to supply missing services is necessary only at early stages of development and should not be carried on longer than

---

BOX 5.2 TYPES OF INFORMATION
USEFUL IN DETERMINING THE NATURE OF
FLOWS

Information Mainly from the Central Bank

■ Purchases and sales of spot foreign exchange by the central bank, including line items for passive transactions and active intervention and other activities (foreign exchange department)
■ Swap and forward transactions of the central bank, including values and rates (foreign exchange department)
■ Purchases and sales of foreign exchange by banks from the central bank (foreign exchange department)
■ Comparative tables of domestic interest rates and selected foreign interest rates, including U.S., European, Singapore, and Tokyo rates, distinguishing between short-term and long-term rates (research department)
■ Relative inflation rates for selected countries
■ Real exchange rate appreciation and volatility (research department)
■ Information on major banking and

capital market regulatory changes that may allow access to the United States, Japan, or other markets (bank supervision department and securities regulatory agency)

Information Mainly from Banks

■ Short-term foreign exchange deposits of nonresidents in banks
■ Short-term local-currency bank deposits of nonresidents in banks
■ Short-term foreign exchange and local-currency deposits in authorized capital market subcustodian banks
■ Forward and swap transactions of banks, including values and rates
■ Interbank foreign exchange transactions, including type, rates, and values
■ Off-balance-sheet foreign exchange assets and liabilities of banks, including guarantees
■ Value of foreign-exchange-denominated assets and liabilities of banks
■ Net open foreign exchange positions of banks, distinguishing between on-balance-sheet and off-balance-sheet positions, by currency
■ Bank loans for equity purchase and to securities companies

---

needed. Prolonged government intervention can inhibit the development of real market institutions and involve the government in costly financial operations.

5. An example of this type of government or regulatory failure is the savings and loan crisis in the United States. Nearly unlimited deposit insurance allowed savings and loan institutions to seek funds for risky projects without facing market scrutiny. Stiglitz (1994) argued that this kind of government failure could be avoided if regulations were better designed.

6. China has been actively pursuing the listing of companies on overseas exchanges. On August 4, 1994, the State Council passed a Special Regulation on Corporations Issuing and Listing Shares Overseas. On the same day, Shandong Huaneng Power, Inc., successfully listed its stocks on the New York Stock Exchange, with a

- Bank loans for land and building purchases
- Borrowings by banks abroad, source, value, maturity, currency, interest rate, and type of loan
- Lending interest rate spreads among selected countries
- Deposit interest rate spreads among selected countries

Capital Market Data from the Securities Regulatory Agency and the Stock Exchanges

- Purchases and sales of equity and debt on securities exchanges by foreign investors, distinguishing between institutional and individual transactions
- Information (in advance) of timing, value, allocation method, and subscription dates of specific public equity offerings
- Information (in advance) of timing, value, allocation method, and subscription dates for specific bond offerings
- Information on derivatives
- Price-to-earnings ratios on stock markets
- Total new issues, market capitalization, trading volume, and value on securities market

Other Capital Market Data

- Equity and debt public listings abroad, by name of exchange, currency, time, and type, with relevant details (reporting requirement for listing companies)
- Large-scale private placement abroad (reporting requirement)

Information from Nonbank Financial Institutions

- Foreign assets and liabilities of nonbank financial institutions, including leasing, factoring, insurance, and pension funds, as relevant
- Sources and uses of funds of nonbank financial institutions (obtained from regulatory bodies)

Data on Foreign Direct Investment

- Foreign direct investment flows, including approvals and actual flows, by project type and currency (obtained from regulatory bodies)
- Foreign direct investment flows into financial sector companies, by type of company

Other Data

- Terms of trade for major commodities

---

stable share price. It raised $333 million in capital. One of the factors contributing to this success was the upgrading of accounting and audit rules.

7. An important consideration in this area is the extent to which countries ought to allow universal banking, under which commercial banking and securities and investment banking activities are merged, or require a separation of these functions. There are strong views on both sides. The debate is beyond the scope of this book and is best left to national authorities to decide.

8. In the long run, direct public deposit insurance for small savers is probably a desirable exception to this general approach. Such schemes should be transparent and funded through fees, probably on banks.

9. Rating Agency Malaysia (RAM) is a private company created in November

1990, with shareholders from fifty-one financial institutions—thirty-three commercial banks, six merchant banks, ten finance companies, the Asian Development Bank, and the IFC (see US ASEAN Council 1994, pp. 31, 34).

10. Boxes 5.1 and 5.2 were written by Betty Slade.

Toward a Framework for Managing Capital Flows

Managing capital flows is a complex matter that is closely related to a country's development strategy, market structure, and institutional arrangements. Although both theoretical and practical considerations provide general guidance on issues and real-world constraints, neither offers simple rules or "silver bullets" that lead to easy solutions for policymakers. Policy actions must be country- and situation-specific. Nevertheless, to help guide authorities, a useful framework can be devised that takes into account overall policy objectives, the persistence of capital flows, constraints faced by policymakers, and the potential fragility of the financial sector.

The key development objectives pursued by East Asian governments that are relevant to managing capital inflows can be summarized in their approximate order of priority (recognizing, of course, that they are ultimately interconnected), as follows:

- Encourage high levels of domestic saving and investment in order to achieve broadly based growth

- Promote exports, which are key to sustaining high growth

- Maintain macroeconomic stability and control inflation

- Attract and absorb foreign investment to help growth

- Strengthen financial sectors and develop a domestic capital market

■ Continue liberalization of current and capital accounts.

Overview of Development Issues

Developments in capital markets are intimately linked to broader programs of liberalization of goods markets and financial sectors and to the encouragement of private sector activities. Across the board, countries in East Asia are reducing or eliminating direct controls on their economies in favor of more indirect and market-based management, with rewarding results. The choices in this transition are not easy and add to the complexity of policymaking. Greater openness of capital accounts and the threat of large capital movements reduce the scope of some traditional policies, such as setting interest rates or allocating credit. Understandably, governments are reluctant to compromise the effectiveness of their direct policy intervention tools. Domestic capital markets are not yet fully developed, new tools are not yet fully in place, and transition takes many countries into new territory, which is seen as risky. But the momentum for change is strong. How can these challenges be accommodated in the liberalizing and rapidly growing environment of East Asia?

The specific mix of development policies followed by individual countries has varied (see World Bank 1993a for a more complete discussion). In general, countries in East Asia have tended to manage exchange rates to promote exports. Domestic financial markets have been controlled to encourage investment in industry and in export-oriented activities. Governments have been willing to intervene by using industrial policy to promote development, although the record in this area is mixed. In most countries fiscal policy has been kept balanced and inflation rates have been moderate or low. Financial sector development has been less robust than in the goods sectors, partly because of official involvement, including the use of mild repression—interest rate controls, directed credit, and ownership of financial institutions.

Approaches toward liberalizing the financial sector and opening the economy to external capital flows have varied as widely as other aspects of development policy. Korea and Taiwan (China) are only now cautiously loosening controls on FDI and FPI, after imposing severe constraints on foreign investment during most of their early development period. Indonesia, Malaysia, the Philippines, and Thailand adopted more open postures and welcomed FDI earlier in their development process; they are continuing to liberalize their foreign investment and capital market regimes. Indonesia has significantly expanded the range of domestic assets open to foreign ownership. Malaysia has completed a major strengthening of its financial sector economy. In the Philippines, which recently emerged from the shadow of its commercial bank debt crisis, direct investment is increasing, and the country is attracting more portfolio investment as its market reforms gather momentum. Thailand has been opening its financial sector to more foreign participation while absorbing large FDI flows. China and the countries of Indochina (Cambodia, Laos, and Viet Nam) are just beginning to rely on markets and are moving to encourage foreign capital flows. China has begun dismantling a web of restrictions on foreign ownership of enterprises and on foreign investors' access to domestic capital markets. Viet Nam has just completed a set of basic transition reforms and is viewed as very attractive by a growing number of investors.

The strength of FDI flows has been based largely on attractive production conditions in the recipient countries. The surge in FPI is to a greater extent attributable to developments in source-country markets, primarily low interest rates and the activities of aggressive mutual fund managers in the United States, than to recipient countries' objectives and strategies. As a consequence, FPI has posed more of a management challenge for countries. The decline in FPI flows after the rise in U.S. interest rates and the Mexican crisis led to revised views of emerging markets and reduced portfolio flows. Slower FPI flows have no doubt been a relief to many East Asian countries, although they have had to grapple with sharp short-term outflows in some cases. As emerging markets become more integrated into global investment portfolios, they can expect to be subject to greater ebb and flow of interest-sensitive instruments as a function of changing interest rates in the United States and, to a lesser extent, in Japan.[1]

The general trend toward indirect controls has occasionally been interrupted in periods of short-term stress because countries have retained the option to use direct intervention selectively where necessary. Indonesia has restricted foreign borrowing when it appeared that it would overheat the economy, and Malaysia recently felt compelled to impose direct controls on foreign transactions. These measures caused strong reactions in the market, and controls were dismantled after the threat had passed. East Asian countries used both direct and indirect policies in the aftermath of the Mexican crisis and have so far successfully avoided contagion. It is important to assure investors that application of these policies is indeed temporary. Both quick action and caution are required. Surges in capital inflows can overheat the real economy, disrupt the financial sector—leading to asset inflation and speculative bubbles—and result in currency appreciation, which would slow the export drive that is the primary growth engine for these countries. There is always a danger that some sectors of the economy will see an advantage in continuing restrictive policies, to the detriment of longer-term efficiency. Inept interventions can also lead to distortions that have negative long-term consequences for growth. So far, disturbances have been contained in East Asian countries. The challenge is to continue to absorb the flows productively while pursuing growth objectives.

Deficiencies in domestic financial markets still plague most East Asian economies but have been partially compensated by the availability of offshore financial channels and the ease of using them to carry out some intermediation. Both the regional centers (Hong Kong and Singapore) and the international markets have been used and continue to play an important role. They have provided an important safety valve for the current influx of capital into the region, easing pressure on domestic markets and increasing investor confidence. Intermediation through regional centers improves capital allocation among countries in the region and provides important economies of information gathering and dissemination.

Instruments for Managing Capital Flows

Policymakers have a number of instruments for managing capital flows. Some of the more direct measures, such as setting interest rates, directing credit, limiting foreign ownership of assets, requiring registration and approval of investments, and segmenting capital markets, fall under the rubric of controlling capital flows rather than managing them. The ongoing process of liberalization is dismantling these controls because they tend to be inefficient, create costly distortions, and are generally contrary to the trend toward more open and integrated markets. Nevertheless, some controls remain in place in East Asian countries, and authorities may regard them as the ultimate recourse in times of crisis, as do industrial countries.

Governments are turning to more indirect instruments to advance their policy aims and to ensure that markets are stable and well functioning. Although perhaps less precise in immediate impact, these methods disrupt economic efficiency much less than the direct controls they are replacing. Learning how to use the new policies effectively and being willing to accept the apparently lower precision that may result are important parts of the transition. (In fact, the actual results of direct controls are often less precise than they initially appear, since secondary reactions, distortions, and evasions may undermine the expected results.) The shift toward indirect policies is an essential element of developing more market-oriented economies in order to realize the benefits of greater efficiency and to gain access to world capital markets. Integration into world markets means that factors beyond the control of the authorities will have a larger effect on outcomes, but governments in East Asia can still exercise a great deal of influence if they take a consistent and positive policy stance and make their policies clear to the markets. Effective use of indirect measures also requires the development of deep, stable, and well-regulated domestic capital markets. Authorities have at their disposal a number of market-based tools for managing capital flows. The selection of specific tools and extent of their application will depend on individual country circumstances. (See box 6.1 for a brief summary of policy options.)

However obvious, it is important to emphasize that East Asia's governments must not falter or backslide on the basics. They must not let inflation get out of hand, allow budget deficits to grow, let savings decline, distort markets, allow large divergences between domestic and foreign interest rates, or try to impose direct controls on capital flows (save in clear emergencies). East Asian countries have done well in these respects, but they cannot relax. There is scope for further reform in most areas. Nostalgia for a simpler world of intervention and of isolation from global markets should be avoided. Capital flows have already changed the outlook and policies of the largest recipient countries. In addition, recipients of foreign investment need to provide for return flows when foreign investors eventually decide to repatriate profits and capital.

Short-Term Policies

STERILIZATION AND MONETARY POLICY. Countries in East Asia have resorted to sterilized intervention in the first instance to counteract the effects of recent capital flows. Purchasing foreign exchange and issuing domestic bonds (or carrying out any equivalent series of transactions) to absorb the liquidity thereby created help to prevent rapid expansion of the money supply and to protect the exchange rate from appreciation. This buys the government time to consider other options, but it may be expensive. Governments usually earn less on the reserves they acquire by this method than they pay on the bonds they issue; for example, Indonesia's Central Bank paid over $1 billion to sterilize short-term flows in 1992–93. Furthermore, sterilization under a fixed exchange rate regime tends to keep interest rates high, which is likely to be counterproductive.[2] It also increases the degree of risk faced by the central bank, which bears the exchange risk of holding the foreign currency that is sterilized.

Sterilization is not a sustainable policy when capital inflows are persistent, and countries have eventually backed away from it. A recent IMF study of recipients of sharp increases of capital flows in Latin America and East Asia indicates that in the first year after an upsurge in capital inflows, about half the flow is sterilized, but the degree of sterilization declines sharply thereafter as other measures are put in place and the country adjusts to accommodate the sustained higher level of inflows (Schadler and others 1993). Sterilization has

BOX 6.1 TOOLS FOR MANAGING CAPITAL FLOWS

Sound macroeconomic policy keeps inflation under control, encourages productive investment, and minimizes distortions in both internal and external transactions. Within such a framework, authorities have a wide variety of tools for managing capital flows. Indirect instruments are consistent with overall liberalization programs and are generally more effective than direct interventions.

Long-Term Policies

■ Macroeconomic policy balance that favors relatively tighter fiscal policy and somewhat more relaxed monetary policy
■ Liberalization of external and domestic trade
■ Positive investment climate, with minimal restrictions on foreign ownership of assets
■ Promotion of high domestic saving
■ Relatively wide intervention bands on the exchange rate, with periodic revisions if needed
■ Support for a strong financial sector, with foreign participation
■ Sound prudential regulation and enforcement in financial and capital markets
■ Free capital movement in both directions
■ Collection and dissemination of information by rating agencies and other means
■ Reduction or elimination of government financial guarantees
■ Encouragement of private hedg-

ing markets, with adequate prudential regulation

Short-Term Policies for Dealing with Precipitous Flows

■ Sterilization of "excess" inflows
■ Higher reserve requirements for banks (on all transactions or on foreign transactions)
■ Limitations on open foreign exchange positions of financial institutions
■ Informal pressure by authorities on the financial markets
■ Foreign borrowing limits on classes of liabilities or public borrowers
■ Taxes on short-term foreign borrowing
■ Restrictions on foreign ownership of certain short-term assets
■ Restrictions on certain speculative transactions

The short-term policies tend to impose costs on the financial system; if maintained for too long, they may lead to distortions as bad as the ills they are supposed to cure. They are primarily designed to help governments react to sharp changes in capital flows and buy time to assess more fundamental causes and cures. The farther down the list, the less desirable the policy, and the sooner it should be reversed. If such policies cannot be reversed in a reasonable time, more fundamental changes are needed in other policies. As countries develop, maintain high rates of growth, and continue to attract capital, gradual appreciation of the exchange rate should be expected.

been shown to be more effective in East Asia than in Latin America, in part because asset holders in the former have greater confidence in government policy and are more willing to hold bonds. When current account deficits are allowed to increase to help absorb the capital inflow, the capital account surplus requiring sterilization operations is lower, easing pressure on reserves and the exchange rate. Malaysia and Thailand have allowed current account deficits to increase substantially to help absorb large capital flows.

With open capital accounts and fixed exchange rates, the scope of monetary policy in general is limited. It is harder to sustain interest rate differentials in relation to international markets (give or take any country and exchange risk premiums). This limits the range of independent monetary policy actions a country can effectively use. Reducing interest rates may reduce the country's attractiveness to interest-sensitive portfolio flows but is likely to result in the expansion of domestic credit, which could lead to real appreciation, an investment boom, or an appreciation of assets, including real estate. If this results in overheating, monetary contraction would be in order, reducing investment but possibly attracting portfolio flows by high interest rates. Furthermore, when firms are increasingly able to borrow abroad, directly or through local banks, they can skirt domestic credit restraint and may further complicate the government's policy agenda.[3] Borrowing abroad can be particularly worrisome if firms are financing abroad to meet working capital needs or to finance speculative real estate investments. Clearly, monetary policy actions must be carefully balanced with other policy measures. To a certain extent, the discipline imposed by external capital markets should be a relief to authorities, since it can counter pressure from special interests for interventions in their favor.

RESERVE REQUIREMENTS AND OTHER TACTICAL RESPONSES. An alternative to sterilizing increases in liquidity from capital inflows is to increase reserve requirements for commercial banks. This lessens the expansionary effects of the inflows and reduces the direct cost to the government, but it adds to bank intermediation costs, which will be passed on to the public. Lower deposit rates may lower returns to portfolio investors, discouraging further inflows but perhaps also lowering domestic savings. However, if domestic borrowing costs rise, borrowers may seek funding overseas, especially in regional capital markets.[4] Another option is to ban or set limits on the net open foreign exchange positions of commercial banks, where they are allowed to hold foreign exchange. By balancing their foreign exchange positions, banks are forced to use offsetting foreign exchange assets to buffer net inflows of capital. Various taxes can also be imposed on foreign inflows on the basis of the source, type of instrument, or maturity. Short-term borrowing may be subject to a tax whose level declines with maturity, increasing the cost to the borrower and lowering the return to the lender. Transactions in capital markets may be taxed where foreign flows are involved. Returns may be taxed differentially for foreign and domestic-held instruments, or some transactions may be controlled.

These measures reduce the real return on investment and are usually intended to deter short-term flows. Together with other regulatory and administrative procedures, they inconvenience and intimidate would-be investors and impose economic costs on the investor and on the economy. They may slow flows without basically changing the market's fundamental structure or investors' incentives. Discriminatory policies of this type are likely to be hard to apply owing to difficulties in identifying the nature of the flows and the many possibilities of disguise. They also require extensive information about individual transactions, which is often unavailable in East Asian and other emerging markets. These policies tend to be most useful as a short-run response to sudden changes in normal flows that appear to be driven by speculative bursts and when they do not introduce large rent-creating distortions. They cannot, however, be the basis of sound long-term strategy. Even if they are not evaded (as they will be if there are high potential returns), they are likely to disrupt financial sector reforms in the long term. Experience has also shown that it is easier to control short-term inflows than outflows. Where short-term flows are responding to unsustainable distortions in prices or other variables, the capital movements should be read as a signal to the government to get its policies back in line; they should not be stifled because they are inconvenient. One possible guideline would be that any emergency measure to counteract undesirable short-term flows should be reversed in a short period of time—say, three to six months. If the measure cannot be removed within that time, it is a sign that fundamental problems in the policy regime need to be corrected.

EXCHANGE RATE POLICY. Increasing the range of permitted exchange rate movements increases the risks faced by international investors and tends to reduce incentives for capital flows, particularly short-term speculative flows. East Asian countries have tended to manage their exchange rates either to be stable or to decline at a fairly predictable rate. Coupled with relative domestic price stability, this policy has been effective in encouraging FDI and promoting exports by assuring investors of a stable exchange regime on which to base decisions. But it has also offered foreign investors—long-term and short-term alike—an implicit guarantee on the part of the exchange risk. A reasonable amount of flexibility in monetary policy can be maintained by broadening the intervention bands on the exchange rate and forcing short-term investors to face more uncertainty (see, for example, Sensson 1992). If exchange rate fluctuations are relatively short term and have the property of mean reversion to a central rate or trend—a reasonable expectation in East Asian economies, which have long-term records of stability—a surprising amount of short-term room for monetary policy maneuvering can be attained by widening the intervention bands. Short-term exchange rate fluctuations will likely tend to discourage speculative flows but will not significantly deter FDI or long-term portfolio investment, provided that the fundamentals remain in place. Wider bands also furnish the government more market-based information on the exchange rate and policy effects because there is more variation in the market rate to analyze.

Long-Term Policies

TRADE AND INVESTMENT POLICIES. In the longer term, a broader policy response than the measures outlined above is required. Absorbing the *additional* flows and directing them into productive additional investment is critical. The protectionist measures used in the past to "develop" certain sectors and promote industrialization are likely to be less effective and to create distortions that speculators can take advantage of. On the other hand, trade liberalization, domestic market reforms, and liberalized investment policies, which are desirable for a variety of reasons and are being pursued throughout East Asia, facilitate the absorption of capital flows by allowing the real transfer of inflows and reducing pressure on the real exchange rate. Sustained capital inflows should help continue or even accelerate these reforms as the balance of payments constraint usually encountered by such reforms is eased. As Malaysia and Thailand have demonstrated, large current account deficits can be maintained with rapid export growth and high levels of foreign investment. However, unless the increase in net imports contributes to greater productive capacity and increased future exports, a country may face problems in meeting its external liabilities down the road. Thus trade liberalization needs to be accompanied by appropriate investment policies that encourage efficient investment in productive sectors.

CAPITAL MARKET REFORM. Deeper and better-functioning capital markets will facilitate the absorption and management of large inflows. Liberalization of domestic capital markets will also help sustain capital flows, especially portfolio flows. Development of these markets is vital to governments' ability to manage and absorb the capital flows and, more broadly, to manage their own economies through indirect measures. Development of domestic capital markets requires improvement of the regulatory systems, creation of incentives that promote prudent behavior, and modernization of the basic infrastructure for transactions. International markets are already far advanced in this regard. East Asian markets will have to catch up in order to remain attractive, particularly to long-term investors, who are the most valuable. Capital market reforms will increase the recipient country's attractiveness to foreign investment and improve the allocation of resources so as to enhance growth. Tax and regulatory policies should support these changes.

FISCAL POLICY. Countries can also counteract the unwanted impacts of large capital inflows, such as excess demand and real exchange rate appreciation, by constraining fiscal policy. Such actions as running a smaller public deficit or shifting to a surplus on the government's consolidated budget would have a relatively stronger effect under a fixed exchange rate regime (either real or nominal), which most East Asian economies have. Malaysia and Thailand have managed tight fiscal positions over several years as part of major reforms. Although these programs were not specifically designed to offset the impacts of capital flows, they did help in that regard. Sound fiscal policy and sustainable deficits, however defined, are to be heartily recommended in general. But that is different from using fiscal adjustment to counteract capital inflows, an approach that may be problematic. The speed of response that is possible through a change in the budget stance is one concern; it is relatively easier to shift monetary policy in the short term than to change fiscal stance. Central banks can intervene in markets to raise or lower interest rates or money supply in a matter of days, or less, and even announcements of policy intentions can have an effect in more developed (and more sensitive) markets. This is perhaps one reason for the initial preference for sterilized intervention: changing the fiscal balance takes longer.

Since middle-income East Asian countries generally do not have a large public sector, the opportunity for undertaking easy reforms to reduce the net deficit may be limited. Budgets are usually established on an annual basis and carry considerable political baggage. Actual budget implementation is under the control of a variety of agencies that cannot quickly fine-tune their revenue or expenditure patterns. Indeed, even in times of severe budgetary crisis, reducing the net deficit has proved difficult. In contrast, the economies in transition do have large public sectors, which they are working to reduce. This involves not only efforts to reduce expenditures on a wide variety of categories, including transfers to SOEs, but also efforts to privatize many SOEs and so reduce the government's overall investment in the economy. Privatization will help reduce pressure on public budgets and deepen capital markets. The more restrained the public sector deficit, the easier it will be for the country to absorb external capital, and the less the inflationary pressure.

On the expenditure side, East Asian countries face growing demands for infrastructure investment, as well as continued expenditures on human resources, and it is not easy to argue that major cuts are desirable. Unfortunately, budget reductions usually fall on investment—the key to sustained growth. In Thailand fiscal contraction included reducing infrastructure spending, which contributed to deficiencies in that sector. East Asian countries are becoming more active in trying to attract private and foreign investment into infrastructure, not so much to replace public investment as to supplement it. On the revenue side, to the extent that a stable and supportive fiscal environment helps attract foreign investment, efforts to raise taxes would tend to reduce that flow, depending on the kind of taxes imposed. Obviously, consumption taxes would be more conducive to investment than income or capital taxes. Much of Thailand's revenue gains, for example, came from increasing revenues through a value added tax.

Put simply, tightening fiscal policy as a response to private capital inflows involves substituting *foreign private* demand for *domestic public* demand (consumption or investment) when public expenditures are cut, or substituting *foreign private* demand for *domestic private* demand when revenues are raised. These considerations suggest that any fiscal response would have to be implemented over the longer term as part of a widely accepted evolution of public policy. This approach would make sense if the capital flows were expected to be persistent and relatively nonvolatile around a given level or trend.

That said, the foregoing analysis makes clear that a macroeconomic policy mix consisting of relatively tighter fiscal policy and looser monetary policy is more likely to be sustainable in the face of open capital accounts and potential capital inflows than the opposite weighting. Fiscal constraint tends to increase national saving and create space for the demand resulting from foreign capital inflows. It also gives the government more room to maneuver in the event of capital outflows. Monetary relaxation encourages domestic investment and growth and offers less inducement for short-term capital inflows. Conversely, looser fiscal policy is likely to increase domestic consumption, and tight monetary policy (higher interest rates) will tend to reduce investment and encourage interest-sensitive capital inflows. This combination may not be sustainable.[5] In either case the scope for monetary actions will be constrained by the openness of capital accounts and the substitutability of assets.

INVESTMENT ABROAD. Given the recent influx of capital inflows, it is not surprising that attention has been primarily focused on how to manage and absorb them. But as East Asian countries become more integrated into global markets, a broader perspective on managing flows in both directions should be adopted. Concern over capital flight and rapid reversal of flows is legitimate. Large flows can reduce domestic saving and impair development, as the experience of Latin America has demonstrated. The situation in East Asia, however, is different. Saving and investment rates are high, and the trade and production structure of these countries is bringing them into an increasingly complex network of international transactions. The volume of capital flowing in on a long-term basis is more than even these fast-growing countries can efficiently absorb. It would be normal in these circumstances to expect some private capital to flow abroad, and that is beginning to happen.

Successful world-class firms (as indicated by very competitive exports) would have many reasons to expand production abroad. The high and rising level of FDI among East Asian developing countries is already witness to this trend. Indeed, there is evidence that entrepreneurs from most countries in the region are investing more widely in both developing and industrial countries. Even in domestic investment portfolios, there are good reasons to expect some holdings of foreign assets. Domestic markets are often relatively small, and domestic investors can improve their risk-return profiles by investing abroad, just as investors in the United States and elsewhere are gaining from diversifying their portfolios into emerging markets. Growth of pension funds in most of these countries will provide some additional demand for international portfolio diversification (see box 6.2 on Chile's experience). Taiwan (China) is currently the source of over $1 billion a year of portfolio investment abroad. China is already investing more than $300 million a year abroad, and that figure is growing rapidly.[6] Malaysian entrepreneurs are actively investing abroad, and Hong Kong capitalists are investing in U.S. real estate. From a national point of view, it makes sense to encourage these flows to improve a country's overall risk exposure and reduce the pressure of capital inflows on exchange rates and domestic capital markets.

Authorities need to treat capital accounts like current accounts and adjust policies to encourage efficient flows in both directions so as to achieve an overall balance consistent with long-term development objectives. No single component should be treated in isolation. Because distortions in any market affect other markets, the aim of policy should be to reduce distortions in both capital and goods markets in a coordinated manner while preserving stability.

The Challenge Ahead

Although looking into the future is always a risky business, some things are likely to be good bets. Rapid growth is likely to continue in East Asia, and the pace of change experienced by these economies should continue to be very impressive. East Asian economies are committed to an open and cooperative approach in the evolution of economic relations among themselves and with the rest of the world and will use market-based and competitive means to achieve their goals. Several observations can be made concerning the future of capital flows.

BOX 6.2 CHILE'S PRIVATE PENSION FUNDS

Starting in May 1981, Chile undertook a revolutionary reform of its bankrupt public social security system and replaced it with a private pension fund system. The original "pay-as-you-go" public pension system was in deep financial trouble, with deficits amounting to 5 percent of GDP in the early 1980s. It was replaced by a fully funded pension system based on individual capitalization accounts, which are government mandated and regulated but privately managed by specialized companies known as Administradoras de Fondos de Pensiones. Participation in the new system is compulsory for all employed workers, including civil servants, but optional for self-employed people. At the beginning of the reform, participation was optional for members of the old system. Thus the new system coexists with the old system, which serves retirees and workers who did not switch.

The pension fund system has grown steadily, and its success is multidimensional. Here we focus on its contribution to capital market development.

■ The pension fund has become a major source of private sector savings, accounting for 18.8 percent of national savings in 1990 and 35 percent in 1994. Contributions are rapidly increasing: annual contributions reached 7 percent of GDP in 1994, up from 1.9 percent in 1982. Total funds accumulated in personal pension plans grew at a real rate of around 40 percent a year, reaching a stock of $22.3 billion, equivalent to 43 percent of GDP, by the end of 1994.

■ Pension funds play an important part in the financial markets. At the end of 1994 the system held 55 percent of all state securities, 11 percent of equities, 59 percent of corporate bonds, 62 percent of all mortgage instruments, and 9 percent of local currency deposits.

■ Since 1990, pension funds have been allowed to own foreign assets and have begun actively to diversify into international capital markets. By the end of 1994 about 3 percent of total assets had been invested outside Chile, and the amount is growing.

Chile's success in pension reform shows the important role domestic savings institutions can play in aggregating small private savings, supporting the development of a domestic capital market, and raising aggregate savings. Furthermore, as these saving pools have expanded and come to own a large share of domestic assets, they have been allowed to diversify abroad, reducing their risk and offsetting other capital inflows into Chile. This represents an important expansion and deepening of Chile's capital markets and its further integration into global markets.

Sustainability

Substantial capital flows into East Asian countries will persist, absent major international crises or domestic policy reversals. The dynamism and success of the East Asian economies will ensure their continuing attractiveness for investment. It is estimated that nearly one-third of world growth will occur in East Asia over the next decade, and global investors will not want to miss out on such opportunities (World Bank 1994a). East Asian countries are gaining greater access to major capital markets, and investors in capital-rich countries are expanding their horizons and including more emerging market issues in their portfolios. The demand for investment opportunities in East Asia has tended to exceed the absorption capacity of some countries, leading to sharp increases in reserves. This situation may not persist, but assuming that these countries sustain high growth and maintain open markets, they will be able to attract funds. For the reasons discussed earlier, the volumes, types, and destinations of capital flows are likely to vary over time as a result of developments in suppliers' capital markets, political events, or technological change.

Greater Integration

The integration of East Asian economies into world markets will continue. On the one hand, integration of national capital markets into global markets offers a number of economic benefits to East Asian economies, the most important of which is access to vastly larger amounts of capital that can further development. Foreign capital inflows also provide technology, assistance in developing local capital markets, and access to foreign markets for exports. On the other hand, greater integration into global markets reduces the degree of domestic policy independence East Asian economies can exercise. Authorities will have to rely on different and more indirect policy tools, continue liberalizing, strengthen domestic capital market structures, and exercise greater supervision of capital markets.

Risk Management

Exposure in external markets, whether public or private obligations, brings a variety of risks that need to be recognized and properly provisioned for. Risks—exchange rate risk, interest rate risk, credit risk—vary among assets. Often, individual borrowers do not take into account the exchange rate risk or leave it implicitly to the government.[7] Where risk-hedging instruments exist, they have potential to allow agents to increase as well as to reduce risk—the Barings Bank episode demonstrates how risks can be magnified. Investors need to understand that they are exposed to these risks, without public guarantee, and they need to understand the nature of the risks. One of the disciplines of market liberalization is to allow agents to take losses or fail. Unless governments permit this discipline, it is hard to make reforms credible. Furthermore, the aggregation of individual actions by many actors in smaller markets may create systemic risks, even though each action is "reasonable." When domestic banks borrow heavily abroad to lend locally, they act as brokers and assume all the exchange and intermediation risks in a single direction. The country, as well as the banks, may be exposed if domestic performance or external conditions change. Similarly, if many individual agents independently undertake foreign obligations, their joint actions may create a risky situation for the country—too much exposure in a single currency or market, for example. The growth of futures markets and other hedges makes it easier and less costly for arbitrageurs and speculators to "bet" against central bank actions on interest or exchange rates.

As countries and individual investors become more integrated into global capital, they will have to learn to manage market risks in a much broader sense. Access to foreign markets gives governments and agents within a country a wider range of instruments for investment and risk management. This allows diversification of balance sheets beyond a country's initial endowment set, through bringing in investment in other kinds of capital and allowing the country and its nationals to own assets abroad.[8] For example, recent yen appreciations have increased debt service substantially for both public and private borrowers in many East Asian countries, and, as a result, some borrowers are shifting the mix of their assets to include more yen. Access to international markets also allows a country to reduce the adverse impacts of external shocks by giving it a resource cushion in addition to diversification. Although international asset-liability diversification would allow a country to increase its growth potential and manage or reduce traditional risks, such benefits can only be achieved if countries and agents within the country act prudently. International markets expose a country to new and potentially larger risks and offer investors some tempting, but risky, gambles.[9]

Where markets are maturing and integration is still incomplete, governments have a responsibility to oversee capital flows and forestall systemic risk factors. Financial markets have special properties that make it easy to argue for government intervention to avert or mitigate systemic crises. Appeals for special treatment, however, should be resisted. In particular, unpriced guarantees (implicit as well as explicit) should be avoided. In large part, appropriate education, information dissemination, positive incentives, and prudential regulations should help avoid systemic problems. Incentives and prudential regulation can be structured to discourage particularly risky behavior or excessive borrowing. Governments may also encourage markets to develop their own risk-management instruments, with private agents absorbing more of the risk. Allowing national investors, including national pension funds, to invest more abroad also helps reduce overall country risk, as well as the risks faced by individual investors. Ultimately though, authorities have some responsibility for helping manage the country's exposure in external markets, and they have to take this responsibility into account in their planning.

Information

Unfortunately, as capital markets and flows are liberalized, the traditional sources of data about capital flows—permits and registrations, for example—have diminished. Reducing direct intervention and controls increases, rather than reduces, the need for information. Individual agents have a greater range of choices and therefore need more, and more reliable, information to make efficient choices.[10] This is particularly true for foreign investors. Use of indirect policies must be based on detailed information about what is going on in the markets and what the reactions to policy actions are likely to be. Good policymaking requires a great deal of empirical research to understand the functioning of individual markets and the impacts of specific policies. This need for information and for its analysis is one reason why good central banks tend to have the best economic research staffs—as they should.

Procedures should be put in place to record and make available in a timely fashion relevant information about capital flows and their impacts on the financial sector, including the banking system. Indicative lists of such information were supplied in boxes 5.1 and 5.2. In most countries, enough information exists to shed some light on the types and volumes of capital moving in and out and on the primary motivating factors, but this information may not be readily available to policymakers or private decisionmakers. Greater efforts to compile these data will be vital to the continued liberalization of capital markets and the effective management of capital flows. It would also make life easier for analysts trying to better understand the impacts of such flows. The importance of timely and relevant information for managing capital flows and averting systemic crises cannot be emphasized enough. Often, small reactions early in a sensitive situation can be much cheaper and more effective than a more massive intervention later. Early action is possible only if authorities have correct information on time.

Conclusions

To manage capital flows effectively, East Asian countries will need to coordinate policies. The sustainability of capital flows depends on maintaining good macroeconomic and sectoral policies and promoting continued rapid growth, which in turn depends on continuing liberalization and integration into international markets. Domestic reforms, especially in capital markets, will increase both integration and the country's ability to deal with large capital flows. At the same time, these reforms will limit the authorities' policy independence and constrain them to maintain key macroeconomic variables close to world levels. The domain of viable policies will shift to more indirect instruments. Greater exposure to world markets increases the variety of risks a country's portfolio position may be exposed to, but world markets also offer more ways to manage and reduce that risk. Authorities need to be aware of the risks and how to manage them. Governments will have to reckon with increased information costs. Indirect policies are based on managing markets through a variety of incentives that can only be properly set if adequate information about transactions and market trends is available.

Critical factors to keep in mind when governments face a potentially large capital inflow are how much of the flow can be absorbed and is therefore likely to be sustainable and how much is a response to short-term factors that are not sustainable and may turn out to be volatile or reversible. An understanding of the relation of domestic to international market factors helps in making this determination, as does knowledge of the flow's type and characteristics. Since there is no way to know accurately investors' intentions or expectations, authorities will have to make their best guesses and be prepared to revise them in light of new information. Depending on their analysis of the flow, authorities should try to determine how much of it supports policy objectives, whether the implications for domestic saving and investment are acceptable, whether there are sectoral constraints that need to be addressed, and whether the capital flow is the result of a mismatch between domestic and international policies on interest rates or other variables. From this analysis the government should derive policy responses: closer alignment of domestic and international interest rates, changes in incentives to reduce short-term inflows or outflows, alleviation of sectoral bottlenecks in trade or finance, sterilization for a period to protect the exchange rate, acceptance of more exchange rate movement, or promotion of longer-term adjustments in public and private (or both) savings behavior. If markets fail to respond as desired to the initial policy response, the authorities should be prepared to change course quickly.

Although experience so far indicates that East Asian governments are responding well to the challenge, they will have to continue their policy reforms and adjustments. Once embarked on this road, countries cannot turn back if they want to maintain their growth rates. East Asia is rapidly becoming part of the industrialized and highly interlinked world. Indeed, the region is becoming one of the engines of global growth—and the implication is that East

Asian countries will have to shoulder greater responsibilities in the international economic system.

Notes

1. Small shifts at the margin in the large markets can generate flows that are large in relation to the size of emerging markets. These flows are seeking high short-term financial yields, not physical investment, and recipient countries should view them accordingly.

2. Short-term flows are most sensitive to interest differentials, and these funds are least productive for the recipient economy.

3. If domestic deposit rates are not particularly high or if there is uncertainty about domestic policy, foreign short-term money might not flow in because of the interest rate differential, but domestic firms might try to finance themselves abroad, where borrowing rates are, or appear to be, lower.

4. Increasing reserve requirements and similar policies in effect shift some of the sterilization burden to the banking sector, along with the attendant risks and costs. Depending on how robust the banking system is, this shifting may or may not be desirable.

5. In Mexico the large inflow of foreign capital essentially substituted for domestic savings, so that consumption rather than investment increased. A large quasi-fiscal deficit and relatively high interest rates also contributed to the crisis.

6. The figure refers to recorded direct investment overseas. The magnitude of other capital outflows is discussed in box 2.1.

7. Foreign lenders are not above insisting that the government ultimately guarantee the exchange rate risk on private transactions. It is widely believed that the Chinese government will do so for nonguaranteed Chinese borrowing abroad, even though the government has strongly asserted that it will not. It may be hard for governments to resist when their international credit standing, as well as that of the private borrower, is threatened, as happened to some Latin American countries during the debt crisis.

8. Think of Indonesia as naturally long in oil, Singapore and Hong Kong as long in human capital, and Thailand as long in rice production capacity, with each facing the associated risk exposure of those positions. Investment in other assets, manufacturing at home, or other assets abroad can diversify these risks.

9. There has been ample recent experience with borrowers and investors who have been caught failing to manage risks or mismanaging them because of incomplete understanding of the market and its instruments. Malaysia's 1992 loss in currency transactions is one example; the 1994 bankruptcy of Orange County, California, is another.

10. After the December 1994 crisis, a number of foreign investors in Mexico complained about the lack of early-warning data from the government and from international sources.

Appendix Tables

All tables are based on World Bank (1996). The table number corresponds to the number of the matching text figure.

APPENDIX TABLE 1.1   NET CAPITAL FLOWS TO DEVELOPING REGIONS, 1970–94
(billions of dollars)

Region	1970	1975	1980	1985	1990	1991	1992	1993	1994
East Asia	2.2	7.2	13.2	15.7	28.9	34.5	53.4	73.2	85.3
South Asia	1.4	4.0	6.6	7.3	9.4	10.9	9.3	10.1	13.8
Sub-Saharan Africa	1.7	5.7	15.1	8.7	17.1	16.3	16.3	13.5	20.1
Latin America and the Caribbean	4.2	15.4	29.9	15.2	21.5	30.3	34.4	64.2	51.1
Middle East and North Africa	1.2	9.1	8.3	14.8	9.9	11.5	7.5	9.1	10.3
Europe and Central Asia	0.7	2.9	15.3	7.5	15.1	23.2	34.2	37.2	26.8
Total	11.3	44.2	88.4	69.4	101.9	126.8	155.1	207.3	207.4

Note: Figure 1.1 is based on this table.

APPENDIX TABLE 2.1   NET PRIVATE CAPITAL FLOWS TO DEVELOPING REGIONS, 1970–94
(billions of dollars)

Region	1970	1975	1980	1985	1990	1991	1992	1993	1994
East Asia	0.8	4.7	8.9	10.9	20.4	26.1	44.7	62.9	77.3
South Asia	0.1	0.2	1.2	2.4	2.4	2.1	2.8	4.6	7.4
Sub-Saharan Africa	0.8	2.3	7.9	0.0	0.2	1.0	0.3	–0.8	4.7
Latin America and the Caribbean	3.2	12.5	24.6	7.3	12.2	22.6	30.3	58.8	49.7
Middle East and North Africa	0.6	3.4	–1.2	6.8	0.5	2.3	0.4	3.8	4.1
Europe and Central Asia	0.3	2.3	11.9	5.3	8.2	7.1	21.6	25.0	15.6
Total	5.8	25.4	53.3	32.7	44.0	61.5	100.3	154.3	158.8

Note: Data for figures 1.2 and 1.3 are calculated on the basis of this table and Appendix table 1-1.

APPENDIX TABLE 2.2   NET COMMERCIAL BANK LENDING TO DEVELOPING REGIONS,
1970–94
(billions of dollars)

Region	1970	1975	1980	1985	1990	1991	1992	1993	1994
East Asia	0.5	2.8	5.0	1.1	4.7	6.0	8.8	–3.9	3.4
South Asia	0.0	0.0	1.0	1.7	1.7	0.2	1.8	0.8	–0.6
Sub-Saharan Africa	0.1	0.4	3.2	–1.9	–0.7	–0.6	–2.1	–0.7	0.1
Latin America and the Caribbean	1.5	8.7	16.5	2.7	2.9	1.5	4.8	–0.1	5.5
Middle East and North Africa	0.0	0.8	0.3	1.7	–1.4	1.7	–0.2	–1.4	1.8
Europe and Central Asia	0.3	1.4	6.2	3.1	–5.4	–6.3	0.6	0.4	–1.0
Total	2.3	14.2	32.2	8.3	1.7	2.5	13.8	–4.9	9.2

APPENDIX TABLE 2.3   FOREIGN DIRECT INVESTMENT IN DEVELOPING REGIONS, 1970–94
(billions of dollars)

Region	1970	1975	1980	1985	1990	1991	1992	1993	1994
East Asia	0.3	1.0	1.3	3.2	11.0	13.9	21.7	37.9	43.0
South Asia	0.1	0.1	0.2	0.3	0.5	0.5	0.6	0.8	1.2
Sub-Saharan Africa	0.4	1.1	0.0	1.0	0.9	1.8	1.5	1.8	3.0
Latin America and the Caribbean	1.1	3.3	6.1	4.4	7.8	12.6	14.5	15.7	20.8
Middle East and North Africa	0.3	1.7	–3.3	2.0	2.8	1.8	2.1	3.8	3.7
Europe and Central Asia	0.1	0.2	0.7	0.6	2.1	4.4	6.3	8.3	8.4
Total	2.3	7.4	5.1	11.3	25.0	35.0	46.6	68.3	80.1

Note: Data for figures 2.3 and 2.4 are calculated on the basis of this table.

APPENDIX TABLE 2.4   DISTRIBUTION OF FOREIGN DIRECT INVESTMENT TO DEVELOPING
COUNTRIES, 1970–94
(percent)

Region	1970	1975	1980	1985	1990	1991	1992	1993	1994
East Asia	11.8	13.9	25.9	28.1	43.9	39.7	46.5	55.5	53.7
South Asia	3.0	1.5	3.6	2.3	1.9	1.3	1.3	1.2	1.6
Sub-Saharan Africa	18.8	14.9	0.7	8.4	3.5	5.2	3.2	2.6	3.7
Latin America and the Caribbean	48.1	44.4	120.6	38.6	31.4	36.0	31.0	23.0	26.0
Middle East and North Africa	13.0	23.2	–65.0	17.4	11.0	5.2	4.5	5.5	4.6
Europe and Central Asia	5.3	2.1	14.3	5.2	8.4	12.6	13.5	12.2	10.4
Total developing countries	100.0	100.0	100.0	100.0	100.0	100.0	100.0	100.0	100.0

Note: Calculated on the basis of Appendix table 2.3.

APPENDIX TABLE 2.5   NET TOTAL PORTFOLIO INVESTMENT IN DEVELOPING REGIONS,
1980–94
(billions of dollars)

Region	1980	1985	1990	1991	1992	1993	1994
East Asia	0.2	4.5	2.5	4.4	7.9	26.6	25.8
South Asia	0.0	0.3	0.4	1.4	0.2	2.5	6.4
Sub-Saharan Africa	1.5	–0.4	–0.9	–0.5	0.2	–1.4	1.7
Latin America and the Caribbean	0.8	–0.8	1.2	10.4	13.0	45.0	25.9
Middle East and North Africa	0.0	0.8	–0.1	–0.1	–0.2	–0.7	–0.3
Europe and Central Asia	0.0	1.1	3.6	4.6	6.0	12.1	7.7
Total	2.6	5.5	6.7	20.4	27.2	84.0	67.1

Note: Includes both bond placement and portfolio equity investment.

APPENDIX TABLE 2.6   BOND PLACEMENT BY REGION, 1980–94
(billions of dollars)

Region	1980	1985	1990	1991	1992	1993	1994
East Asia	0.2	4.3	0.2	3.3	2.8	8.5	13.2
South Asia	0.0	0.3	0.3	1.4	–0.2	0.5	0.2
Sub-Saharan Africa	1.5	–0.4	–0.9	–0.5	0.1	–1.6	0.8
Latin America and the Caribbean	0.8	–0.8	0.1	4.1	4.7	19.8	12.7
Middle East and North Africa	0.0	0.8	–0.1	–0.1	–0.2	–0.7	–0.4
Europe and Central Asia	0.0	1.1	3.4	4.6	6.0	11.9	5.7
Total	2.6	5.4	3.0	12.8	13.2	38.3	32.2

APPENDIX TABLE 2.7   NET PORTFOLIO EQUITY INVESTMENT BY REGION, 1980–94
(billions of dollars)

Region	1980	1985	1990	1991	1992	1993	1994
East Asia	0.0	0.1	2.3	1.0	5.1	18.1	12.6
South Asia	0.0	0.0	0.1	0.0	0.4	2.0	6.2
Sub-Saharan Africa	0.0	0.0	0.0	0.0	0.1	0.1	0.9
Latin America and the Caribbean	0.0	0.0	1.1	6.2	8.2	25.1	13.2
Middle East and North Africa	0.0	0.0	0.0	0.0	0.0	0.0	0.1
Europe and Central Asia	0.0	0.0	0.2	0.0	0.1	0.2	1.9
Total	0.0	0.1	3.7	7.6	14.1	45.6	34.9

Selected Bibliography

Agenor, Pierre-Richard, and Nadeem U. Haque. 1994. "Macroeconomic Management with Informal Financial Markets." IMF Paper on Policy Analysis and Assessment. International Monetary Fund, Washington, D.C.

Akerlof, G. A. 1970. "The Market for Lemons: Quality Uncertainty and the Market Mechanism." *Quarterly Journal of Economics* 84(3, August): 488–500.

Allen, Polly Reynolds. 1991. *Open Economy Macroeconomics: A Review Essay.* London: Elsevier Science Publishers.

Allen, Polly Reynolds, and Jerome L. Stein. 1991. "The Dynamics of the Real Exchange Rate, Foreign Debt and Capital Intensity." *Journal of Monetary Economics* 27: 151–56.

Arrow, Kenneth J., and Michael D. Intriligator. 1981–91. *Handbook of Mathematical Economics.* Amsterdam: North-Holland.

Asian Development Bank. 1993. *Asian Development Review: Studies of Asian and Pacific Economic Issues* 11(1).

Bekaert, Geert. 1993. "Market Integration and Investment Barriers in Emerging Equity Markets." In Stijn Claessens and Sudarshan Gooptu, *Portfolio Investment in Developing Countries.* World Bank Discussion Paper 228. Washington, D.C.

_____. 1995. "Market Integration and Investment Barriers in Emerging Equity Markets." *World Bank Economic Review* 9(1): 75–107.

Bencivenga, Valerie, Bruce Smith, and Ross Starr. 1995. "Equity Markets, Transaction Costs, and Capital Accumulation: An Illustration." Paper presented at the World Bank Conference on Stock Markets, Corporate Finance, and Economic Growth, February 16–17, Washington, D.C. World Bank, Research Advisory Staff, Washington, D.C.

Bercuson, Kenneth, and Linda Koenig. 1993. "The Recent Surge in Capital Inflows to Asia: Cause and Macroeconomic Impact." SEACEN/IMF Seminar, Seoul, Republic of Korea. International Monetary Fund, Washington, D.C.

Bernstein, Peter L. 1987. "Asset Allocation: Things Are Not What They Seem." *Financial Analysts Journal* (March–April): 636–38.

Blommestein, Hans J., and Michael G. Spencer. 1993. "The Role of Financial Institutions in the Transition to a Market Economy." International Monetary Fund, Research Department, Washington, D.C.

Boyd, John H., and Bruce D. Smith. 1995. "The Co-Evolution of the Real and Financial Sectors in the Growth Process." Paper presented at the World Bank Conference on Stock Markets, Corporate Finance, and Economic Growth, February 16–17, Washington, D.C. World Bank, Research Advisory Staff, Washington, D.C.

Buckberg, Elaine. 1995. "Emerging Stock Markets and International Asset Pricing." *World Bank Economic Review* 9(1): 51–74.

Calvo, Guillermo A., Leonardo Leiderman, and Carmen Reinhart. 1994. "Capital Inflow Problems: Concepts and Issues." *Contemporary Economic Policy* 12 (July): 54–66.

Caprio, Gerard, Jr., Izak Atiyas, and James A. Hanson, eds. 1994. "Financial Reform: Theory and Evidence." World Bank, Policy Research Department, Washington, D.C.

Cho Soon. 1994. *The Dynamics of Korean Economic Development.* Washington, D.C.: Institute for International Economics.

Cho, Yoon-Je, and Deena Khatkhate. 1989. *Lessons of Financial Liberalization in Asia: A Comparative Study.* World Bank Discussion Paper 50. Washington, D.C.

Chuhan, Punam. 1994. "Are Institutional Investors an Important Source of Portfolio Investment in Emerging Markets?" Policy Research Working Paper Series 1243. World Bank, International Economics Department, Washington, D.C.

Chuhan, Punam, Stijn Claessens, and Nlandu Mamingi. 1993. "Equity and Bond Flows to Asia and Latin America: The Role of Global and Country Factors." Policy Research Working Paper Series 1160. World Bank, International Economics Department, Washington, D.C.

Claessens, Stijn. 1995a. "Corporate Governance and Equity Prices: Evidence from the Czech and Slovak Republics." Paper presented at the World Bank Conference on Stock Markets, Corporate Finance, and Economic Growth, February 16–17, Washington, D.C. World Bank, Research Advisory Staff, Washington, D.C.

_____. 1995b. "The Emergence of Equity Investment in Developing Countries: Overview." *World Bank Economic Review* 9(1): 1–17.

Claessens, Stijn, and Sudarshan Gooptu. 1993. *Portfolio Investment in Developing Countries.* World Bank Discussion Paper 228. Washington, D.C.: World Bank.

Claessens, Stijn, and Rhee Moon-Whoan. 1994. "The Effects of Barriers on Equity Investment in Developing Countries." Policy Research Working Paper Series 1263. World Bank, International Economics Department, Washington, D.C.

Claessens, Stijn, Susmita Dasgupta, and Jack Glen. 1995. "Return Behavior in Emerging Stock Markets." *World Bank Economic Review* 9(1): 131–51.

Claessens, Stijn, Michael P. Dooley, and Andrew Warner. 1995. "Portfolio Capital Flows: Hot or Cold?" *World Bank Economic Review* 9(1): 153–74.

Cline, William R. 1995. *International Debt Reexamined.* Washington, D.C.: Institute for International Economics.

Cole, David C. 1993. *Financial Sector Policies of Selected DMCS Financial Reforms in Four Southeast Asian Countries: Indonesia, Malaysia, Philippines and Thailand.* Cambridge, Mass.: Harvard University Press.

Corbo, Vittorio, and Leonardo Hernández. 1994. "Macroeconomic Adjustment to Capital Inflows: Latin American Style versus East Asian Style." World Bank, International Economics Department, International Finance Division, Washington, D.C.

Dadush, Uri B., Ashok M. Dhareshwar, and Ronald Johannes. 1994. "Are Private Capital Flows to Developing Countries Sustainable?" World Bank, International Economics Department, Washington, D.C.

Dalla, Ismail, and others. 1992. "Philippines Capital Market Study." 2 vols. Report No. 10053-PH. World Bank, East Asia and Pacific Country Department I, Washington, D.C.

Dalla, Ismail, and others. 1993. "Korea Financial Sector Study." Report No. 11373-KO. World Bank, East Asia and Pacific Country Department I, Washington, D.C.

Dallara, Charles H. (managing director, Institute of International Finance). 1994. Letter to Minister Philippe Maystadt, Chairman of the World Bank–IMF Interim Committee. Institute of International Finance, Inc., Washington, D.C.

Das Gupta, Dipak, and Bejoy Das Gupta. 1994. "Interest Rates in Open Economies: Real Interest Rate Parity, Exchange Rates, and Country Risk in Industrial and Developing Countries." Policy Research Working Paper Series 1283. World Bank, East Asia and Pacific Country Department III, Washington, D.C.

Demirgüç-Kunt, Asli, and Ross Levine. 1995. "Stock Markets and Financial Intermediaries: Stylized Facts." Paper presented at the World Bank Conference on Stock Markets, Corporate Finance, and Economic Growth, February 16–17, Washington, D.C. World Bank, Research Advisory Staff, Washington, D.C.

Demirgüç-Kunt, Asli, and Vojislav Maksimovic. 1995. "Stock Market Development and Firm Financing Choices." Paper presented at the World Bank Conference on Stock Markets, Corporate Finance, and Economic Growth, February 16–17, Washington, D.C. World Bank, Research Advisory Staff, Washington, D.C.

Dornbusch, Rudiger. 1987. "Open Economy Macroeconomics: New Directions." NBER Working Paper 2372. National Bureau of Economic Research, Cambridge, Mass.

El-Erian, Mohammed, and Manmohan S. Kumar. 1995. "Emerging Equity Markets in Middle Eastern Countries." *IMF Staff Papers* 42 (June): 313–43. Washington, D.C.: International Monetary Fund.

Faruqi, Shakil, ed. 1992. *Financial Sector Reforms, Economic Growth and Stability: Experiences in Selected Asian and Latin American Countries.* EDI Seminar Series. Washington, D.C.: World Bank.

_____, ed. 1993. *Financial Sector Reforms in Asian and Latin American Countries: Lessons of Comparative Experience.* EDI Seminar Series. Washington, D.C.: World Bank.

Fischer, Stanley, Richard C. Marston, J. David Richardson, Jeffrey D. Sachs, and Martin Feldstein, eds. 1988. *International Economic Cooperation.* Chicago: University of Chicago Press.

Flemming, J. M. 1962. "Domestic Financial Policies under Fixed and Floating Exchange Rates." *IMF Staff Papers* 9: 369–70.

Frankel, Jeffrey. 1993. "Sterilization of Money Inflows: Difficult (Calvo) or Easy (Reisen)." Working Paper C93-024. University of California at Berkeley, Department of Economics, Berkeley.

Frenkel, Jacob A., ed. 1988. *International Aspects of Fiscal Policies.* National Bureau of Economic Research Conference Report. Chicago: University of Chicago Press.

Fry, Maxwell J. 1988. *Money, Interest and Banking in Economic Development.* Baltimore: Johns Hopkins University Press.

_____. 1993a. "Current, Lagged, and Differential Effects of Foreign Direct Investment on Saving, Investment, Exports, Imports, and Growth in East Asia and Other Developing Areas." World Bank, International Economics Department, Washington, D.C.

_____. 1993b. "Foreign Direct Investment in a Macroeconomic Framework. Finance, Efficiency, Incentives, and Distortions." Policy Research Working Paper Series 1141. World Bank, International Economics Department, Washington, D.C.

_____. 1993c. "Some Lessons for South Asia from Developing Country Experience with Foreign Direct Investment." Internal Discussion Paper 127. World Bank, International Economics Department, Washington, D.C.

Glen, Jack. 1995. "International Comparison of Stock Trading Practices." Paper presented at the World Bank Conference on Stock Markets, Corporate Finance, and Economic Growth, February 16–17, Washington, D.C. World Bank, Research Advisory Staff, Washington, D.C.

Goldstein, Morris L., and Michael Mussa. 1993. "The Integration of World Capital Markets." *IMF Working Paper*. International Monetary Fund, Washington, D.C.

Goldstein, Morris, David Folkerts-Landau, Peter Garber, Liliana Royas-Suárez, and Michael Spencer. 1993. *International Capital Markets. Part I: Exchange Rate Management and International Capital Flows*. Washington, D.C.: International Monetary Fund.

Gooptu, Sudarshan. 1994. "Are Portfolio Flows to Emerging Markets Complementary or Competitive?" Policy Research Working Paper Series 1360. World Bank, International Economics Department, Washington, D.C.

Greenwald, Bruce C., and Joseph E. Stiglitz. 1992. "Information, Finance and Markets: The Architecture of Allocative Mechanisms." *Journal of Industrial and Corporate Change* 1(1).

Greenwald, Bruce C., Joseph E. Stiglitz, and Andrew Weiss. 1984. "Informational Imperfections in the Capital Markets and Macroeconomic Fluctuations." *American Economic Review* 74(1): 194–99.

Grossman, Sanford J., and Joseph E. Stiglitz. 1980. "On the Impossibility of Informationally Efficient Markets." *American Economic Review* 70(3, June): 393–408.

Hanna, Donald P. 1994a. *Indonesian Experience with Financial Sector Reform*. World Bank Discussion Paper 237. Washington, D.C.

_____. 1994b. "What Drives Interest Rates in Indonesia and Are They Too High?" East Asia and Pacific Regional Series. World Bank, Washington, D.C.

Harvey, Campbell R. 1995. "The Risk Exposure of Emerging Equity Markets." *World Bank Economic Review* 9(1): 19–50.

Howell, Michael. 1993. "Institutional Investors and Emerging Markets." In Stijn Claessens and Sudarshan Gooptu, *Portfolio Investment in Developing Countries*. World Bank Discussion Paper 228. Washington, D.C.

Husain, Ishrat, and Kwang W. Jun. 1992. "Capital Flows to South Asian and ASEAN Countries: Trends, Determinants and Policy Implications." Policy Research Working Paper Series 842. World Bank, International Economics Department, Washington, D.C.

IFC. 1994. *Emerging Stock Markets Factbook 1994*. Washington, D.C.: International Finance Corporation.

_____. 1995. "Quarterly Review of Emerging Stock Markets, Second Quarter." Washington, D.C.

IMF. 1995a. *International Capital Markets. Part II: Systemic Issues in International Finance*. Washington, D.C.: International Monetary Fund.

_____. 1995b. "International Capital Markets: Developments, Prospects and Policy Issues." International Monetary Fund, Washington, D.C.

_____. Various issues. *International Financial Statistics*. Washington, D.C.: International Monetary Fund.

Ishaq, Ashfaq. 1994. "Boots Projects for the Third World: Boon or Bane?" Paper presented at a seminar sponsored by the Society for International Development. USA International, Washington, D.C.

Ishii, Shogo, and Steven Dunaway. 1994. "Portfolio Capital Flows to the Developing Country Members of APEC." International Monetary Fund, Policy Development and Review Department, Washington, D.C.

Japan External Trade Organization. 1993. "Foreign Investment in the PRC, 1991–92." *China Newsletter* 102 (January–February): 16.

Jones, Ronald, and Peter Kenen, eds. 1985. *Handbook of International Economics*. Vol. 2. New York: North-Holland.

Kawaguchi, Osamu. 1994. "Foreign Direct Investment in East Asia: Trends Determinants and Policy Implications." Internal Discussion Paper 139. World Bank, East Asia and Pacific Region, Washington, D.C.

Keynes, John Maynard. 1919. *The Economic Consequences of the Peace*. Cambridge, U.K.

Khan, Mohsin S., and Carmen M. Reinhart. 1994a. "Economic Management in Maturing Economies: The Response to Capital Inflows." Paper presented at the Asia-Pacific Economic Cooperation (APEC) Finance Ministers Meeting, September 26, Honolulu, Hawaii. International Monetary Fund, Research Department, Washington, D.C.

_____. 1994b. "The Effect of Capital Inflows on the Domestic Financial Sectors in APEC Developing Countries." Paper presented at the Asia-Pacific Economic Cooperation (APEC) Finance Ministers Meeting, September 26, Honolulu, Hawaii. International Monetary Fund, Research Department, Washington, D.C.

Kim, E. Han, and Vijay Singal. 1993. "Opening Up of Stock Markets by Emerging Economies: Effect on Portfolio Flows and Volatility of Stock Prices." In Stijn Claessens and Sudarshan Gooptu, *Portfolio Investment in Developing Countries*. World Bank Discussion Paper 228. Washington, D.C.

King, Robert G., and Ross Levine. 1992. "Financial Indicators and Growth in a Cross-Section of Countries." Policy Research Working Paper Series 819. World Bank, Financial Sector Development Department, Washington, D.C.

_____. 1993. "Finance, Entrepreneurship and Growth." Working Paper. World Bank, Policy Research Department, Washington, D.C.

Korajczyk, Robert A. 1995. "A Measure of Stock Market Integration." Paper presented at the World Bank Conference on Stock Markets, Corporate Finance, and

Economic Growth, February 16–17, Washington, D.C. World Bank, Research Advisory Staff, Washington, D.C.

Kueh, Y. 1992. "Foreign Investment and Economic Change in China." *China Quarterly* 131(September): 637–90.

Levine, Ross. 1994. "Government Insurance and Financial Intermediaries: Issues of Regulation, Evaluation, and Monitoring." In Shakil Faruqi, ed., *Financial Sector Reforms, Economic Growth and Stability: Experiences in Selected Asian and Latin American Countries*. EDI Seminar Series. Washington, D.C.: World Bank.

Levine, Ross, and Sara Zervos. 1995. "Policy, Stock Market Development and Long-Run Growth." Paper presented at World Bank Conference on Stock Markets, Corporate Finance, and Economic Growth, February 16–17, Washington, D.C. World Bank, Research Advisory Staff, Washington, D.C.

Marston, Richard C. 1985. "Stabilization Policies in Open Economies." In Ronald Jones and Peter Kenen, eds., *Handbook of International Economics*. New York: North Holland.

————. 1988. *Misalignment of Exchange Rates: Effects on Trade and Industry*. A National Bureau of Economic Research Project Report. Chicago: University of Chicago Press.

Mathieson, Donald J., and Liliana Rojas-Suárez. 1993. *Liberalization of the Capital Account: Experiences and Issues*. IMF Occasional Paper 103. Washington, D.C.: International Monetary Fund.

McKinnon, Ronald I. 1993. *The Order of Economic Liberalization: Financial Control in the Transition to a Market Economy*. 2d ed. Baltimore: Johns Hopkins University Press.

Mintz, Jack, and Thomas Tsiopoulos. 1993. "Taxation of Foreign Investment in South Asia." Internal Discussion Paper 135. World Bank, South Asia Region, Washington, D.C.

Montiel, Peter J. 1993. "Capital Mobility in Developing Countries: Some Measurement Issues and Empirical Estimates." Policy Research Working Paper Series 1103. World Bank, International Economics Department, Washington, D.C.

Mundell, R. A. 1963. "Capital Mobility and Stabilization Policy under Fixed and Flexible Exchange Rates." *Canadian Journal of Economics and Political Science* (29): 475–85.

————. 1994. "Capital Mobility and the Relation between Saving and Investment Rates in OECD Countries." *Journal of International Money and Finance* 327–42.

Quirk, Peter J. 1994. "Capital Account Convertibility: A New Model for Developing Countries." International Monetary Fund, Monetary and Exchange Affairs Department, Washington, D.C.

Ramaswami, Sita. 1993. "Indonesia: Non-bank Financial Sector Study." Initiating Memorandum. World Bank, East Asia and Pacific Country Department III, Washington, D.C.

Robinson, David, Yangho Byeon, and Ranjit Teja, with Wanda Tseng. 1991. *Thailand: Adjusting to Success: Current Policy Issues*. IMF Occasional Paper 85. Washington, D.C.: International Monetary Fund.

Schadler, Susan, Maria Carkovic, Adam Bennett, and Robert Kahn. 1993. *Recent Experiences with Surges in Capital Inflow*. IMF Occasional Paper 108. Washington, D.C.: International Monetary Fund.

Schmidt-Hebbel, Klaus, and Luis Servén. 1992. "Macroeconomic Response to External and Policy Shocks in an Open Economy." World Bank, Policy Research Department, Washington, D.C.

Schoenfeld, Steven, Edward Stawderman, Amy Conran, and Ziad Baha-Eldin. 1994. "Emerging Futures and Options Markets: An Overview of Issues and Prospects in Developing Countries." International Finance Corporation, Capital Markets Department, Washington, D.C.

Schwarz, Adam. 1994. "Money Matters: Thailand's Banks Face Intense Competition from the Bond Market and Fast Growing Mutual Funds." *Far Eastern Economic Review* (September 7): 64–70.

Sensson, Lars. 1992. "An Interpretation of Recent Research on Exchange Rate Target Zones." *Journal of Economic Perspectives* 6(4): 119–44.

Servén, Luis. 1994. "Capital Goods Imports, the Real Exchange Rate and the Current Account." Policy Research Working Paper Series 1298. World Bank, Policy Research Department, Washington, D.C.

Sheng Andrew, and Yoon Je Cho. 1993. "Risk Management and Stable Financial Structures." Policy Research Working Paper Series 1109. World Bank, Policy Research Department, Washington, D.C.

Stiglitz, Joseph E. 1992. "Some Lessons from the Asian Miracle." Background paper for *The East Asian Miracle*. World Bank, Policy Research Department, Washington, D.C.

————. 1994. "The Role of the State in Financial Markets." *Proceedings of the World Bank Annual Conference on Development Economics: 1993*. World Bank, Washington, D.C.

Stiglitz, Joseph E., and Andrew Weiss. 1981. "Credit Rationing in Markets with Imperfect Information." *American Economic Review* 71(3, June): 393–410.

Tesar, Linda L., and Ingrid M. Werner. 1995. "U.S. Equity Investment in Emerging Stock Markets." *World Bank Economic Review* 9(1): 109–29.

US ASEAN Council. 1994. "Financing ASEAN's Development." Washington, D.C.

Uy, Marilou. 1993. "The Role of Capital Markets and the Role of Government." World Bank, Financial Sector Development Department, Washington, D.C.

Vittas, Dimitri, ed. 1992. *Financial Regulation: Changing the Rules of the Game*. EDI Development Studies. Washington, D.C.: World Bank.

World Bank. 1993a. *The East Asian Miracle: Economic Growth and Public Policy*. New York: Oxford University Press.

————. 1993b. *Sustaining Rapid Development in East Asia and the Pacific*. Development in Practice Series. Washington, D.C.

————. 1994a. *East Asia's Trade and Investment: Regional and Global Gains from Liberalization*. Development in Practice Series. Washington, D.C.

————. 1994b. *World Debt Tables: 1994–95*. Washington, D.C.

————. 1994c. *World Tables 1994*. Baltimore: Johns Hopkins University Press.

————. 1995. *The Emerging Asian Bond Market*. Washington, D.C.

————. 1996. *World Debt Tables: 1996*. Washington, D.C.

Zervos, Sara. 1995. "Industry and Country Components in International Stock Returns." Paper presented at the World Bank Conference on Stock Markets, Corporate Finance, and Economic Growth, February 16–17, Washington, D.C. World Bank, Research Advisory Staff, Washington, D.C.